The

NEWHALL INCIDENT

America's Worst
Uniformed Cop Massacre

by
John Anderson
with Marsh Cassady

Quill
Driver
Books

Clovis, California

Quill Driver Books/Word Dancer Press, Inc.
8386 N. Madsen Avenue
Clovis, California 93611
(559) 322-5917 • Fax: (559) 332-5967

Printed in the United States of America

Quill Driver Books/Word Dancer Press books may be purchased at special prices for educational, fund-raising, business or promotional use.
Please contact:

Special Markets
Quill Driver Books/Word Dancer Press, Inc.
8386 N. Madsen Avenue
Clovis, California 93611
1-800-497-4909

To order another copy of this book please call
1-800-497-4909

Trade Paperback: ISBN 1-884956-01-7 Cloth: 1-884956-09-2

Quill Driver Books/Word Dancer Press, Inc.
Project Cadre:

Shirley Mann
Stephen Blake Mettee
Cindy Wathen
Linda Kay Weber

Library of Congress Cataloging-in-Publication Data

Anderson, John, 1940-
   The Newhall incident :   America's worst uniformed cop massacre / by John Anderson,   with Marsh Cassady.
      p.   cm.
   ISBN 1-884956-01-7 paper, 1-884956-09-2 cloth
   1. Police murders--California--Newhall.   2. Police patrol--Crimes against--California--Newhall.   I. Cassady, Marsh. 1936-
II. Title.
HV8148.N34A53   1998
364.15' 23' 0979493--dc21   98-40994
                                                                             CIP

PREFACE

The Newhall: America's Worst Uniformed Cop Massacre is a true story. Yet it is unlike most true crime books in that there is no mystery, no investigation, no detective work, no need to prove anything. We know from the beginning who the "good guys" and the "bad guys" are. We know the ending, maybe not in exact and specific detail, but in what became of all six men who met in a service station parking lot just before midnight on April 5, 1970. The outcome is known and unalterable.

The book is a story of the coming together of two strong and separate forces set on their paths long before they actually come face to face.

Bobby Augustus Davis and Jack Wright Twining were destined to meet a grievous end at the hands of the police. Conversely, police were destined to meet them—maybe not specifically Roger Gore, Walt Frago, Skip Pense and Mike Alleyn, but police, nevertheless.

Newhall is an attempt at showing the why of both these sides—why Davis and Twining had no alternative but to come to this sort of end; why four CHP officers had no alternative but to confront them face to face.

Though this was not in my mind when I set out to write this book, it has the elements of classic Greek tragedy. It has a cast of men who, because of background, personality and character, are set upon a certain course, or, in fact, two separate courses, that must then cross. In the Newhall tragedy, unlike most, both the collective protagonist, the four CHP officers, and the collective antagonist, Davis and Twining, have tragic flaws that are a result of two sets of men believing in their own invincibility.

Events, personalities and circumstances beginning years before the actual incident pushed both sides toward a deadly confrontation. The tragic flaw for both the protagonist and the antagonist is believing too strongly that they can succeed, that they are invincible, that they need not consider the consequences of their acts.

Because the characters are human beings, neither gods nor men born to nobility, this is a tragedy of common men. It is a tragedy for both the good guys and the bad guys, each cheated out of his potential, each brought to an end without becoming what he might have become. It is a tragedy for the families of five of the six men.

Although it isn't too difficult to think of the protagonist and the antagonist as personifications of good and evil, they were real men, not film heroes or villains. Rather, they each had hopes and prejudices and preferences; they each had doubts and weaknesses; they each had beliefs and strengths.

At times, in fact, the bad guys fought against the roles in which they were cast. Jack Twining tried his best to become a commercial fisherman. Bobby Davis tried his best to enter the medical field. Yet the men that they were forced to become—due to circumstances, environment and personality—compelled them to fulfill their roles in the playing out of good and evil.

Had Twining and Davis been all bad, this would have been an easier book to write.

I have tried my best to present the six major characters in this clash, this convergence of lives, as truthfully as possible.

JOHN P. ANDERSON

April 5, 1970,
Los Angeles County, California

2337 hours

Dispatch: *"Unit 78-8, Newhall CHP."*

Mobile Unit: *"Newhall, 78-8, we're on the five-mile grade. Go ahead."*

Dispatch: *"78-8, we have a reported brandishing of a weapon fifteen minutes ago. A red '64 Pontiac, Cal license Ocean, Sam, Yellow, 8 - 0 - 5, that's OSY 805, south bound on Highway 99 from Gorman area. The driver threatened another driver with a revolver."*

Mobile Unit: *"Newhall, 78-8, 10-4. We copied and we'll watch for it."*

2353 hours

Mobile Unit: *"Newhall, 78-8."*

Dispatch: *"Go ahead to Newhall, 78-8."*

Mobile Unit: *"Newhall, we're behind that red Pontiac now, OSY 805, southbound at the truck scales."*

Dispatch: *"10-4, 78-8. Newhall to any unit in position to assist 78-8. They are behind a suspected 417 P.C. vehicle, southbound Highway 99 at the truck scales."*

Mobile Unit: *"Newhall, 78-12. We'll help. We're just south of there."*

Dispatch: *"10-4, 78-12. Newhall clear."*

2354 hours

Mobile Unit: *"78-12, 78-8. We'll make the stop at the Valencia off ramp. Stand by there, OK?"*

Mobile Unit: *"10-4, 78-8. 78-12 standing by at Valencia off."*

2355 hours

Mobile Unit: *"Hey, 78-12! The Pontiac is turning off on Henry Mayo Drive; now going right onto old '99. We're stopping it at the Standard station by J's Restaurant!"*

Mobile Unit: *"10-4, 78-8. We'll be there in a minute."*

2356 hours

Mobile Unit: *"Newhall, 78-12! 11-99! SHOTS FIRED! J'S RESTAURANT PARKING LOT!"*

Dispatch: *"10-4, 78-12! 11-99! ALL UNITS! 11-99! SHOTS FIRED! J'S RESTAURANT, HIGHWAY 99 AT HENRY MAYO DRIVE!"*

PART ONE
THE PREPARATION

ONE

Like errant billiard balls herded into a rack, the 120 blue-clad cadets of Training Class V-68 snapped to attention. It was 5:45 a.m., August 13, 1968, an hour before the sun would begin to warm the chill Sacramento air. Roger Gore felt stiff both from the temperature and the unfamiliar posture.

In their second day of training at the California Highway Patrol Academy, the cadets had, in a manner of speaking, learned to salute, to march, and to come to attention. All three actions, Roger Gore surmised, would serve them greatly throughout their long careers.

Surreptitiously, Roger glanced right and left. Everyone looked miserable. Maybe he did too. There was no denying he was sleepy, he was cold, and his belly was issuing growling noises that cadets two rows back most certainly could hear. Yet there also was no denying he would rather be here than any other place on earth.

TWO

Groggy with sleep, lulled by the monotonous rhythm of steel wheels on steel tracks and the drone of the diesel engine, Bobby rubbed sleep from his eyes. Jack Wright Twining still slept, head bouncing against the once-white covering fastened with snaps to protect the seat from drool and greasy hair tonic.

A pale sun struggled to burn through darkness and a brown-tinted haze. Not for the first time Bobby wondered at the path that had taken him to this destination. He'd never meant this to be. He was intelligent, better than this. He'd always intended to be law abiding, just as soon as... What? The world treated him better? His parents stopped looking at him as a failure? He got enough money together to start a legitimate business?

At times he felt close to his goal, close to making it in the straight world. Close to settling down with his wife in a nice quiet neighborhood, close to earning the respect he'd never had. The world through the window of the train looked as bleak as the burned out buildings they were passing. It was ridiculous to think he'd ever get a fair shake from life. Maybe at some earlier point...before they forced him to join the military, before he killed that other Marine, before all the robberies.

The harsh ring of a crossing warning roused Bobby from his depressing reverie. They were passing what looked like a gutted apartment house. Was this Watts? he wondered. So what if it was? It made no difference to his life. He glanced once more at Jack. Even in sleep, he never relaxed his guard. As if to confirm Bobby's thoughts, Jack's body jerked and spasmed. The muscles of his jaw stood out as he clenched his teeth.

Bobby yawned. Jesus, he was tired. They'd been on the fucking train for nearly a day. He leaned his head back and closed his eyes. A Glen Campbell hit ran suddenly through his head. "By the Time I Get to Phoenix." Yeah, he thought, she probably would be rising now, his bride of two days. She'd be getting up, dressing, putting on her makeup in front of the bathroom mirror. Soon she'd leave for her job at the phone company.

In the sort of coincidence Bobby knew that life often has, he spied a clock in a drugstore window. A shade after six. That would make it eight in Houston. Or would it be seven? He frowned at the thought of not knowing. Was it one time change or two they'd passed through?

Damn, he missed Carmel. It wasn't fair to leave her so shortly after the wedding. But he'd had no choice. Yet right now, if she still lingered in bed, it would be nice to snuggle his face against the hollow in her neck, to inhale her scent before her morning shower washed it away.

Bobby glanced once more through the window. On its way to Union Station, the train threaded between the back ends of cheaply-built tenement houses, industrial buildings with dirty red bricks and business establishments. Clotheslines, many laden with yesterday's laundry, stretched across otherwise empty space.

He turned back to Jack, awake now, blue eyes drilling holes—or so it felt—right through Bobby's skull.

"Everything okay?" Jack asked, the force of his tone belied by a slight drawl, the kind Bobby had heard all his life but which he'd worked to eliminate from his own speech.

"Yeah." Bobby wished Jack didn't sometimes cause him to feel so rattled. "We're in L. A. Shouldn't be too much longer." Jesus, but Jack's gaze could be unsettling.

Lines of cars idled on surface streets, drivers waiting to enter ramps leading to nearly clogged freeways.

Jack stood, glancing quickly around the car. Only a few other passengers, Bobby observed. All seemed still to be sleeping.

"I'm gonna take a leak," Jack said. "Keep an eye on the bags." He stretched to loosen the muscles of his back, making sure not to reveal the .45 automatic he carried in the waistband of his pants.

"Yeah, okay." Jesus Christ, the guy is paranoid, Bobby thought, again nudged by the fact that he didn't belong with this man, should never have ended up here despite their past associations. Yet, he conceded, if he were to be with anyone in this sort of situation, Jack Twining was the best. Usually as nervous as a cat stalking a sparrow, on a job he was cool as Texas rain.

"Morning, sir."

Startled, Bobby looked up. An elderly porter approached his seat. "Yeah?"

"'Bout fifteen minutes more, and we'll be comin' in. Can I get someone to look after your bags?"

Bobby gave the man an engaging smile and declined the offer.

"What'd he want?" Jack was back, visually checking their luggage.

"Come on, Jack, sit down. Take your first look at California. Not much of a view, I'll admit, but an improvement over yesterday."

"Ain't my first look. 'Cept it was San Francisco. Seen that from a train too. They take prisoners up there by train to send them over to Alcatraz. Least they used to. But I agree."

"What's that?"

"The view." He chuckled. "Even after bein' incarcerated all them years, this is what I think. You can take all that openness, all them miles of nothing, the whole damned Southwestern part of the good old U S of A, and stick it where the sun don't shine."

"I suspect a lot of folks feel that way. So anyhow the porter said we should be pulling in pretty soon now."

"Well, good. I'm antsy to get out of here. Anxious to get things organized."

He gazed down at his hands clasped between his knees and shook his head.

"Something botherin' you, Bobby?"

"Wondering, that's all."

"Wondering?"

"Yeah."

"About what?"

"Wondering what's gonna happen. What's in store for us here?"

Jack laughed. "And you think I'm nervous."

"Hey, man, I didn't mean—"

He laughed again, the tone softer. "Don't let it worry you, Bobby. Things are going to work out fine."

THREE

Jack smiled to himself. Bobby Augustus Davis was a worrier, but maybe that was good. Someone had to make sure of all the details of any job. Even to check on Jack himself. Yeah, he wasn't afraid to admit it, at least in the privacy of his thoughts: He was a little hot-headed sometimes, a little too quick to fly off the handle. It was good he had someone like Bobby as a stabilizing influence.

He stretched out his legs and yawned. Fucking train rides. He hated them, but at least he could sleep away the biggest part. Right in his seat. Not like those fancy folks who paid out extra money to buy a so-called bed that wasn't any better than the beds in the worst maximum security prisons. Well, not that they were any good either! And in that area Jack was an expert. He'd tested out the beds in eight of the nine major federal pens. El Reno, Oklahoma; Petersburg, Virginia; Chillicothe, Ohio; Atlanta, Georgia; Tallahassee, Florida; Lewisburg, Pennsylvania; Leavenworth, Kansas, and that good old California institution called Alcatraz, a few hundred miles distant from where he was right now. The only one he had missed was Terre Haute, Indiana. He wondered if he held some sort of record for being in the most lockups in the shortest amount of time. It wasn't like he was an old con. Hell's fire and damnation, he was just thirty-four. Why if you counted the dozen or so local lockups where he'd done time, it came to a pretty good total. Fact was, he'd spent a goodly portion of his life incarcerated. But he'd made himself a solemn promise. No matter what, he wasn't going back. No matter what the fuck happened, no one was going to lock him up again.

Still and all, the damned train he was riding and all the other trains rolling over all the steel tracks this side of nowhere were a little like a prison—self-enclosed worlds traveling along by their lonesome. That was a good enough reason right there not to like them. Once you bought your ticket and came aboard and the train started picking up speed, you were trapped. Only in those damned westerns with play actors like Gene Autry and Roy Rogers did anyone get away with jumping off trains. In real life, you'd likely end up with a broken neck.

Well, they'd soon be pulling in. And no matter what he told Bobby, he liked California. It was filled with suckers, ready for outsmarting. Still he'd be glad to get off the train.

Not that anyone was looking for him now. Nobody knew him here. Anyhow he was clean. Relatively speaking. He chuckled, causing Bobby to stare. Playing it cool, he shrugged. Let Bobby wonder if he was putting something over on him. Keep him awake, paying attention.

Good old Bobby. When Jack had called him, Bobby was sure surprised. It took Jack a while to get around to doing that though. He'd had nothing but a bad time since his release from the Federal Pen in Tallahassee. He'd been out eleven months now, his longest stretch of free time since he was a pimply kid of sixteen.

When things hadn't worked out, he'd decided to head on out to Texas. He'd come to Houston with just two thoughts in mind—first, to contact his old buddy, and second to set up some big kind of score. He'd arrived tired, clothes wrinkled like they'd been slept in—which, of course, they had. Without knowing much about the city, he ended up in what had to be the worst part of town. He'd walked into a bar and into a phone booth.

Man, he'd been scared right then. Frustrated and angry, mad at the whole fucking world. Needing cash, needing to get back at all the sons-of-bitches who'd screwed up his life, and not least of all, needing a friend he could trust.

The phone rang five, six times before Bobby answered.

"Hey, man, you know who this here is?"

"Jack? Jesus, it's been a right good spell." He paused. "Is it really you?"

"Who the hell did you expect?" Jack answered, mostly amused but a little bit pissed that Bobby would ever doubt that he'd call. "You don't think I keep my promises?"

"Hey, man, I'm sorry. Didn't mean to cast aspersions."

"Cast aspersions? You swallowed a dictionary or what?"

"That's funny, Jack. I mean you're the guy who taught himself all the big words."

Suddenly, Jack had felt something relax inside. This, after all, was Bobby, the guy he'd taken under his wing before he could come to grief at the hands of the other cons. "Yeah, the same old Jack. I mean we did promise to keep in touch, am I right?"

"It's good to hear your voice."

"Good to hear yours, too." He paused for a minute. What did he know about Bobby anymore? It had been a while, and maybe he'd changed. "So tell me what you've been up to."

"Tried a little of this, and a little of that. I wanted to go to school. Tried to get located where I could do that. Take the classes I wanted, I mean. But they wouldn't have any of it."

"The parole officers?"

"Who else? Hey, where are you, man? You aren't in town?"

"Thought you'd never ask. I'm right here at—" He stuck his head outside the booth and called to the bartender. "What's the address here?" he asked. He listened to the answer and relayed the information to Bobby.

"Just around the corner," Bobby said. "I'll be there in a jiffy."

"I'll be looking for you." He was glad they'd made contact. Bobby was his only real friend, the only man in the whole wide world he was sure he could rely on. And he needed someone like that. He had big plans, and Bobby was just the man to help him carry them out.

The engineer applied the air brakes, and the train screeched to a halt. Bobby stood up. "Southern California. Sand and sunshine. Think they're ready for us here, Jack?"

"Don't know, Bobby. Don't much care. But I know I'm ready for them."

FOUR

As the American and California State flags finally climbed the pole, Roger felt his eyes mist. Damn, what would the other guys think? What would Val think? Big tough Roger Gore, the guy who didn't let anything throw him.

"All right, men. Right HACE! FORWARD HARCH!"

Sunlight bounced off the windshields of the rows of patrol cars parked toward the rear of the Academy.

Instructors already had warned that a lot of cadets would wash out, would be unable to cut it mentally or physically. A few would realize it wasn't for them. Roger was determined to graduate.

He spied Walt Frago up ahead. The officer who investigated their backgrounds had brought them together. Walt had agreed to drive up from Merced. That way Valerie could keep the car. Roger didn't want her stuck somewhere, unable to get to the hospital when the time came.

"Dismissed!"

"What do you say?" Walt asked. "We have some free time. How about a little shuffleboard?"

"I need your advice."

"I'm listening." Walt was slender, sinewy, graceful like an animal. Maybe a buck deer. Though he and Roger were about the same height, Roger outweighed him by at least twenty pounds.

"Got me a bluey."

"What the hell for?"

"Cigarette ashes on my dresser."

"Didn't know you smoked."

"I don't." He was feeling pissed. He didn't want his record blemished. Didn't want to lose the chance to go home during free time. The Academy issued cadets five blue cards. When they screwed up in any way, they had to surrender one of the blueys. When they surrendered all five, they were restricted to grounds.

"So what did you want to ask me?"

"Since it wasn't me who did it, I was thinking of an appeal."

"You asked my advice, Rog."

"Think that would look worse? Is that what you're saying?"

"Do you think you're overreacting? Nobody's out to get you."

"You're sure of that, are you?"

"No, I'm not. But, buddy, you gotta watch that attitude."

"What the hell's wrong...?" He chuckled. "At least I'm going to go back to the dorm and check that it hasn't happened again."

FIVE

Walt could understand Roger's feelings. He was determined to keep his own record clean. There'd be no blueys for him.

At first Walt had been afraid to admit just how much the Academy meant to him. Then on the way up, he and Roger had talked. He found out he wasn't alone. Out of all the guys in the whole damned class, he was willing to bet that nobody wanted to get through any more than he did. And Roger did. He'd decided, however, that he wasn't going to get all uptight about it. Relaxed, easy, that was his approach. Who the hell could focus when he was tense?

He watched as Roger hurried off. They really weren't so different from each other, he thought, despite their approach to life and their physical appearance. Both, he knew, had been taking law enforcement classes before applying to the Academy. Both were married. Walt and his wife had two children. Roger's wife was seven months pregnant.

Ironic, he thought, as he turned and strode toward the mess hall, but the Academy was different from the way he'd figured it. If he were to describe it to Nicki, he'd say the discipline was a little like boot camp must be, the atmosphere like that of a monastery, and the restrictions like those of a prison. He chuckled. "And that," he would tell her, "was looking on the bright side."

• • •

Just before noon Saturday Walt was ready to get on Highway 99 and head on down to Merced. He had his bag packed and was sitting on his bunk waiting for Roger. It would be good to get home. Fifty miles, an hour or so, and he'd be with Nicki and the kids. Maybe they could order pizza from that place off West 16th. Spend the evening curled up on the sofa watching TV.

God, he missed them. They'd always been together, he and Nicki, and had had the two kids well before they were even near to drinking age. Not that he wanted to drink. He didn't, but sometimes life got a little too much with all that responsibility.

To be honest, he had thought that getting away for a little while—not anything permanent—would give him a better outlook. Well, it certainly gave him a *new* outlook anyhow. Damn, he was just as anxious to get home as Roger.

The kids were one and two now, a boy and a girl, and they looked just like Nicki. Had her eyes and her smile. Maybe that's what he missed the most—the smiles.

He glanced up as Roger came through the doorway.

"About time, man," he said. "Thought you were the one so anxious to get back to the mother-to-be."

As they drove off the grounds, Roger turned to Walt. "So what do you think?"

"About the Academy?" Walt nodded. "I think it's going to be okay."

"Me too. Triple A without the tow truck."

Six

How many times had he gone through the same sort of thing, Jack Twining wondered as he walked along toward State Highway 363. From the map he'd seen in the prison library, it looked as if from there he had a good chance of hitching a ride over to Route 267 and on down toward Miami.

It was April, 1969, and he was free—again. His debt to society paid in full. So what? He had nothing to his name, nowhere to go. Should he try to play it straight for a while? Maybe. Maybe he should just go straight from now on. He'd heard that a guy could make a fair living working one of the fishing boats out of Miami. And he'd decided to check it out.

Funny, but even though he hadn't a great deal of actual schooling, he wanted to learn as much as he could. He had an insatiable appetite for learning, almost as strong an appetite as he had for...making it? Having all the money he wanted. Having a good woman. Yeah, but it was the excitement too. Outwitting people who thought they were so damned smart. The establishment. Isn't that what the hippies said? Not that he identified with those weird folks. Not by a long shot. Who did he identify with? Who could he relate to? Hell, he was a loner, maybe with one or two friends. Guys like Bobby. But even with them he never let his guard down completely.

He'd looked it up in the prison library. "Commercial Fishing, Miami, Florida." He could quote the article word for word.

> **Florida rates near the top among states in the value of its annual fish catch. The Gulf of Mexico and the Atlantic Ocean both are major sources of fish. However, each year the Gulf generally proves to bring in approximately twice the profit as the Atlantic. The principal catch includes lobsters, crabs, shrimp, clams, swordfish, oysters, mackerel, red snapper, and mullet.**

What the hell? He didn't have any experience, but he was a quick learner. Could absorb just about anything front to back simply by reading or hearing about it once or by watching someone at work. Like that article on fishing.

He'd fake it. He was damned good at it.

Anything to leave the fucking pen. He was sick of the constant surveillance, the electrified fences and high walls, sick of spending nearly all the time in his damned cell and rarely ever getting outside to exercise. What kind of way was that to treat a human being, for Lord Jesus's sake? And contrary to what the man on the street might think, prisoners *were* human beings. In most cases, the same society that condemned them had been responsible for fucking them up.

It was true, Jack thought. Most nearly every con he'd met had been fucked over by some part of society or another. Family, school, the military. Not being given a decent shot at life. Being stuck in an orphanage or with foster parents who didn't give a fuck about anything except the monthly check the county paid them for taking in kids.

He reached the highway—a sunny stretch of trees and that damned parasitic shit that hung all over them. He stuck out his thumb and waited.

A steady drone of cars roared past, most drivers not glancing his way, till finally this old guy pulled over. An ancient relic in an ancient Fairlane, paint faded to misty grey and bird-shit white.

"Where you headed?" the old man asked as he rolled down the window.

"Miami," Jack said crawling inside. The upholstery was cracked and in places the springs showed. He wondered if the old coot would have stopped if he'd known where Jack was coming from. Not likely!

"Give you a ride down to Highway Nineteen. Far as I'm goin'. That suit you?"

Jack chuckled. "That suits me, old man."

"Still got a long ways after that, boy. Near to 400 miles, I'd guess. But it's a start, ain't it?"

"It's a start," Jack admitted, deciding he liked the guy. Maybe because he reminded him of this other old man—he couldn't remember his name—in one of the many foster homes Jack had bounced into and out of with hardly a stop before ending up with Mrs. Cross. A grandfatherly sort of fellow who lived with his foster parents, if such they could be called.

Jack had liked the old man, one of the few who treated him decently. Even then though, Jack had been afraid. Scared to let go, maintaining an aloofness that kept him apart. Looking back, he felt sad for that kid he was, that unloved kid. He wasn't aloof; leastaways he didn't want to be. It was only that he was shy. A timid little tad, full of bluster as a way of getting through each day. Deep inside he'd been scared shitless, insecure, not ever wanting to face each new morning for fear of what it would bring. And more often than not, the fear had proved not groundless. Not groundless by a long sight.

He kept being sent back to the courts. But that old man had treated him differently, had seen beyond the tough facade and had tried to talk to him. Took him to the park around the corner, spoke to him like he was somebody, not a dumb unwanted discard.

One thing was for sure, Jack thought. It wasn't a facade no more. Everyone, maybe even the old man himself, had interpreted his standoffishness as hostility. Though to the old guy's credit, he did try to bring Jack out of his shell. But it wasn't any use. They prejudged him. Everyone did. Said he was incorrigible. Every damned judge and social worker and police officer just loved that term. A bad kid, nothing but trouble. And so, Jack decided—gradually, when things never got no better—that he might as well have the game as the name.

"Going home?" the driver asked. He had grey hair and a scruffy beard a shade into brown. "Or heading away from home?"

Jack stiffened. What did this old man want? What was his point? He glanced over and caught the guy's glance. Jack saw nothing but interest in the pale blue eyes.

Man, he thought, if I ain't jest paranoid as hell. The old guy was making idle conversation, passing the time.

"Home's much further west."

"Oh, yeah?"

"Texas." Jack glanced out the window. The sun shone on well-kept lawns, palm trees, a mixture of colors in flowers surrounding front porches or hugging fences. "Looking for work," he said.

"What kind of work do you do, young fella?"

"I figure I'll try to hire me on to a fishin' boat. I hear tell they always need help haulin' in them nets."

"I wouldn't rightly know."

"Jest what I heard."

"Though I had some experience myself. Fishin', I mean. Out in California. After I got my discharge from the Navy. Before I decided to come on home to Muncie. Long before I retired and me and the wife moved down here."

Jack sat up and stared at the man. Maybe he could learn a thing or too. "What was it like?"

"Let me tell you. A buddy and I hired on with a tuna boat captain. He had the experience; I didn't. My buddy, I mean. But he put in a good word. Got me a job as a chummer." Blunt fingered hands gripping the top of the wheel, he glanced toward Jack and then back to the road. "Know what that is?"

"No, sir, I don't."

"Chumming is spreading bait to attract fish. The job usually involves cutting the bait too. Hard work but not hard to get onto."

"Tell me about it," Jack said. He leaned his head back and closed his eyes as the old man spoke. By the time Jack stepped from the old guy's car, he knew a hell of a lot more about fishing than the damned article had told him. Practical stuff. Knowledge he could use looking for a job.

• • •

The first thing he did on reaching Miami was get himself a room. The second was to check in with his parole officer, a man named Lanier, who looked to be about sixteen years old and wore glasses with lenses as thick as the bottom of a drinking glass. He wasn't a bad sort though, as such men went. Jack told him about all the reading he'd done concerning the fishing industry and how much he hoped, in whatever small way, to become a part of it.

In less than twenty-four hours Lanier called Jack in and told him he'd set up an interview. Jack said he'd prefer that if and when he got the job, none of the men he worked with knew about his record.

"Is that right?" The parole officer smiled. "A little ashamed of our past, are we?"

Jack felt a flash of anger but pushed it down somewhere inside his gut. "Maybe you could say I don't want to start off on the wrong foot."

"Yeah? Interesting."

"Look, Mr. Lanier. I'm not the begging type. But I ask you, if at all possible, will you work with me on this?"

"Why not? The fewer who know, the better." He glanced at a scrap of paper on the corner of his desk. "Tomorrow morning. Six a.m. Think you can make it?"

"I can make it," Jack said.

"We'll see." Lanier proceeded to give Jack directions on where to go and whom to see.

• • •

He loved the job—the sea, the self-contained world of the fishing boat where he was rarely hassled except sometimes by Murtag, the bastard of a captain, where Jack had nothing to prove except that he could cut and spread bait and help haul in catches.

It was a pretty good life, the best Jack had known. So good, in fact, that he might just want to keep it.

Standing on deck, facing into the wind, he laughed. Who would have thought it? Certainly not any of those foster families. They expected the worst, and that's what he'd showed them. Now he'd show them the other side, the side that could make it in the straight world, a side he was sure none of them knew existed.

The sea was calm, the sun casting liquid gold in the troughs between the waves. This was the life, Jack thought. It made a man feel insignificant with nothing between him and the rugged elements of nature. Yet there was a sense of belonging, of being a part of the whole. And that was good. Jack was tired of being the square peg. The work was hard, but it did his soul good. He knew he was finished with seeking the quick, easy buck. He pretty much had what he wanted now, except...some day he might like to own his own boat. Hell, a whole fleet of his own boats.

Jack often wondered if his ancestors were tied to the sea. He had loved her from his first glimpse years past. He was a born mariner, he thought, a man who had brine in his blood from the day of his birth. To him the sea was a mistress, loving and benevolent, but one who could turn harsh and unyielding. Jack chewed on the thought and then reconsidered. Perhaps the sea was no man's mistress, but rather a siren who lured men to her, demanding respect and devotion. For if a man really loved her, she rarely led him to doom. Most often it was those who discounted her terrible power and took foolish risks who learned too late she would claim them. It would take a lifetime to know her well, Jack thought, but he was prepared to dedicate that lifetime to her.

Maybe he loved the sea so much, Jack thought, loved her because her moods often matched his own. Like her, he had an anger that roiled always somewhere below his consciousness. Like her, he could be placid or jittery or at the right time even playful, though few had seen that mood. He respected her and her moods, just as he himself deserved respect, as every man deserved respect. Yet, he conceded, he'd done very little throughout his whole damned life to earn it. But maybe he was earning it now. He was doing a good thing in turning his life around, and he felt good about it.

He laughed. Okay, man, don't let yourself get carried away with this shit, he thought. Thousands, millions, of other men were doing the same as he in holding honest jobs. For this he deserved a pat on the back? Well, at least it proved he could change, could put aside his old ways and accept the new, just like the Bible spoke of putting away the old man for the new. Not that Jack knew much about the Bible, except for being force fed bits of it now and again in foster homes. Still and all, he liked the feeling of earning his money through backbreaking work, work that covered his palms in calluses.

"Yeah!" he shouted, laughing with the mirthful, shining water that stretched to the far horizon. It was a good time. For him, for the boat. They'd hauled in net after net of fish and were heading back to port with a fucking good catch.

"Hey, man!"

Suddenly tense, Jack spun around but saw it was Gonzalez. José María Gonzalez.

"What you want, man?" Jack asked, adapting his friend's bantering tone.

"Why you standin' here alone? The catch is good. Is time to celebrate."

"What do you think I'm doin', Joey?"

"How the hell do I know what weird gringo thing you're up to?"

"Celebrating. That's what I'm doing."

"Staring out at the water. Lotsa fun, no? Big party all by yourself."

"More ways than one to celebrate. But...on the other hand, I could use a drink or two."

"Sí, have a couple of cervezas. Even the captain is joinin' the fiesta."

"You talked me into it."

"Your first big catch. Your first pay. Is important."

"The first pay of many, my friend."

• • •

"Fucking son-of-a-bitch!"

"Hey, man, what gives?"

Jack and one of the other Cubans, a man named Armando, stood facing toward the dock. It was evening, a cool breeze blowing in over the water, the sun just starting its rapid descent to the far horizon. He might have known things were too good to last.

"Nothin', man."

"Could have fooled me."

"Leave it be!"

"Okay, fine." A muscular man in his fifties, Armando backed away, palms up in apology. "Far be it from me to interfere. Far be it from me to express concern at seeing a guy upset over what looks like nothin'. Mind my own friggin' business."

"I'm sorry. You're right; it was stupid to react that way."

The other man shrugged.

"It's just...." Hell, Jack thought, how was he going to explain. "Thought I saw someone I knew," he said. "On the dock. Someone I want to avoid."

"A jealous husband perhaps. Ah, my friend, I understand."

In spite of himself, Jack laughed.

"See," the man replied. "Things are not so bad."

"Maybe," Jack said, but he was pretty certain they were that bad. He'd spied two men in suits. Dark suits and ties. Only two sorts of people dressed like that and hung around the docks. Big-time narcotics smugglers and the Man. And the drug dealers didn't go around asking questions.

So far the cops hadn't glanced toward the boat. Warily, Jack helped unload the catch. So far, so good. Maybe he was being paranoid. Maybe the Man wasn't after him. He'd served his time, kept himself clean since his release.

Jack helped wash down the boat and then hung around while everyone else went ashore. Maybe he was clean, but he didn't want to be questioned either. He hadn't told anyone he was an ex-con. He didn't want them to find out now.

It was late afternoon, the last rays of the fading sun bouncing off faintly rippling water. The sea was calm, at rest before the crashing waves of high tide. Might as well get comfortable, he thought. He wanted to make damn sure the feds or whoever had gone back to the wife and kiddies or into their hole or wherever guys like that went. He leaned against sun-warmed wood, pulled out a crumpled pack of Chesterfields and his old Zippo lighter. He lit up, inhaled deeply, and let his back slide down the hull till he was in a sitting position. Just like recreation period in the yard. Except that the view was a mite better.

Damn right it was better. Boats and water and palm trees. A few fishermen dropping lines off a pier. It was peaceful, and Jack felt he was due for some of that peace. He puffed out a smoke ring that floated softly in the still air. He blew a smaller one that hit square in the middle of the first and sailed right through. Smoke rings. Shit! He shook his head. Why couldn't they leave him alone? Hell, yes, they were after him, whatever the reason. And sooner or later they'd catch up.

He finished the cigarette and tossed the butt into the harbor—something he didn't normally do. What the fuck. It wasn't going to work out. Letting his head fall back, he stretched his arms straight out over his knees. So what was he going to do? he asked himself. At the moment he hadn't the slightest idea.

Some time later, his legs cramping, the ends of his fingers tingling from being in the same position too long, he pushed off from the hull of the cabin till his feet were flat on the deck. He stood. It was that in-between time, the sun still casting a ghostlike glow over the water. The time when the world appeared not quite real.

Jack stretched a few times, left the boat and strode down the block to a dingy bar frequented mostly by fisherman and others who worked the docks. Up in the corner a TV blared out a rerun of "Gilligan's Island." How appropriate, Jack thought, for a bar near the water.

He slid onto a stool and ordered a beer.

"Hey, man."

Jack turned to see Gonzalez striding toward him. "Did that hombre catch up to you?"

"What hombre?"

"Asking questions. A *federale* or somethin'. Wanted to talk to everyone on the boat."

"Sit down." Jack patted the stool beside his. "Can I buy you a beer?"

"What, you a rich man now after payday? Okay, I let the rich man buy me a drink."

"No rich man, Joey. Just a schmuck tryin' to be a friend."

"Schmuck? *¿Qué es eso?*"

Jack laughed. "Forget it, man. You want a beer, I'll buy you a beer, long as you buy me the next one."

"Sí, Señor. I'm a little slow. Now I catch on."

"Catch on to what?"

"You get me drunk. Then I'm the one who buys the cerveza."

"You know me better—"

José laughed. "I don' trust too many gringos. But I trust you."

"You're one of the first."

"You feelin' sorry for yourself?"

"Forget it." He faced the bartender, ordered two beers and then turned back to José. "So what about this man asking questions?"

"Where you been, man, you don' know about this?"

"I stayed on the boat."

"You don' get enough of that boat when we're out catchin' fish?"

Jack laughed. "Had me a smoke is all."

"Hell of a big cigar, *como no?*"

"Okay, I was doing some thinking."

"You must have seen this man from the boat. Big hombre with a suit and tie."

"I saw him."

José suddenly peered into Jack's eyes. "Hey, man, that couldn't be why you wanted to stay on the boat, eh?"

Jack sighed. "Maybe."

"You in trouble?"

"I'm not in trouble." The bartender sat the beers in front of them, slopping a little over the side of Jack's glass. Jack slid the glass aside and ran a finger idly through the pale liquid. "At least I ain't done nothin' wrong."

"So why you worry?" José took a long swig and wiped the back of his hand across his mouth.

"You know somethin', Joey?"

"*¿Mande?*"

"You're a worse nag than a mother-in-law."

"A joke, no?"

"You say this man wanted to catch up to me?"

"Not just you. Everyone on the boat. Something about some robbery. A *banco*. Somebody took a lot of money."

"Son-of-a-bitch!" He slammed the glass down.

"Hey, amigo, take it easy."

"Sorry." Jack felt a sliver of fear in his gut and tried to quell it. If they knew about him, knew he'd robbed those banks and served his time, why didn't they come to the boat?

"You all right, amigo?"

"I changed my mind, Joey. You can buy me that beer another time." He stood, grabbed up the change he'd left on the bar, and hurried outside. The air felt warm and prickly, not cool as before. Obviously, someone had told the feds that Jack was working the boats. Well, no one knew except that fucking Lanier. Yeah, and he probably told Murtag, and the son-of-a-bitch was spreading it around.

By now it was all over the docks that he was a bad cat, a man who got his kicks from robbing banks. The fear in Jack's gut flared into panic. What the hell was he going to do?

Fucking Murtag! Why was he spreading this around? Only reason, Jack thought, was to gain notoriety. So he could be known as the man who bossed an ex-con, a murderer. In the world of commercial fishing, there were guys who might look up to a man who could do that.

The panic turned to rage. "Asshole. I'm sure gonna fix his wagon. Him and his big goddamned mouth." As he walked along, Jack worried his lower lip between his teeth. What the hell was he going to do? Kill the fucker, that's what. He set out toward his rooming house, the place he'd planned to leave as soon as he could afford something better. Now he'd be leaving sooner than expected.

He'd wait till tomorrow morning and then go to the boat early. Jump that bastard Murtag as soon as he stepped onboard. Murtag was always early, the Cubans always late. There was nothing to worry about. No one would catch him. And it would be good to waste the son-of-a-bitch. And not just for what he'd done to Jack, but for other reasons too. He treated the Cubans like shit and Jack only a little bit better.

He'd do it all right. Snuff the guy and then head out to sea. A few miles from shore he'd dump the fat shit over the side. The sharks would have a hell of a meal. Jack would take the boat and head on down to the Keys.

By now he was almost back to his room and nearly out of breath from walking so fast. Even his shins hurt. Hell, he thought, it was stupid even to consider killing Murtag. What could the FBI do to him? Ask a few questions? His rage subsided as quickly as it had built.

Ask a few questions, all right. But why ask him? He hadn't done nothing. Hadn't hit any goddamned bank. Well, that's the way it was. He'd heard plenty of guys talk about how the system would never let you go straight once you'd fucked up. No matter how good your intentions. Shit, the FBI probably had some damn unsolved case and was looking for a scapegoat. Why the hell did it matter if they caught the right man or not? They could make a big thing of it. Show how special those special agents were to solve the big crime.

Just like the Mounties, the FBI always got their man. Jack laughed bitterly. Bull *shit*. Maybe they always got some man, whether he was guilty or not. Just somebody whose name would fill the bill, and they could stamp "closed" on the case file. Jack knew that from personal experience.

After he'd robbed the bank of St. John in Maserve, and they'd picked him up in New Orleans, the damned FBI brought the fucking unsolved cases from all over the South to confront him with. And then they'd tried to pressure him into telling them he'd robbed every one of those goddamned banks. It was a whole damned strategy. Get a guy to confess to a bunch of crimes he didn't commit and get a lesser penalty on the one he did.

No, sir, he'd never do something like that. Screw the fucking feds. He wasn't copping out to damned FBI pricks!

Still, things didn't look good. He was up a tree like a damned squirrel, and the feds were holding the rifles. If they wanted him, they'd probably be at his room. There wasn't no escape, so he might as well get it over with. He turned up the walkway to the two-story house and pulled out his key. He stopped midstride. "No!"

He turned and hurried away. Maybe they didn't know where he lived, though it would be a simple thing to ask Lanier. Maybe they did know. Maybe they were just playing their asshole FBI games. Maybe they'd be out on the dock in the morning waiting for him to show up.

He paused by the front gate. He didn't want his dream to end like this, but what choice did he have? One thing was certain, whether they were after him now or not, they would be. And he wasn't about to stick around.

It was dark, streetlights casting a pus-yellow glow on the sidewalk. He had a little money with him, but not enough to last very long. Well, shit, he'd show 'em. Just as he'd decided long ago, he might as well have the game as the name.

There was no turning back.

A restaurant stood nearby, a family place where all these people went, old folks, couples with kids. Usually, they didn't have the best of cars. But that was okay. A beatup heap was less likely to call attention.

He'd made his decision, and though it went against everything he'd wanted, it was as if a burden was lifted. There was no more waiting now, no worrying about who'd find out he was an ex-con. No more worries about being hassled by that bastard Murtag and not being able to talk back because he needed to have the job to please Lanier.

His step almost jaunty, he headed for Smith's Family Fare, two blocks south and one block east. It was a little late for dinner hour, Jack thought, but the parking lot was nearly half full. He headed for the far side of the lot, couched in dark shadows. He spied a Chevy, a faded green. Jack laughed sardonically. Not that it mattered, either the make or the color. It was an old car, a '62 or '63, Jack guessed, though he wasn't that much up on cars. Mrs. Cross had had a Chevy, a '58 or '59. This looked a little newer.

Jack had broken into plenty of cars, one of the easiest things on earth. Jimmy the wind wing. Hot wire the car. It took him less than two minutes. He climbed inside, glanced furtively toward the door to the restaurant, saw no one, and gunned the motor. If luck were with him, he'd be a good piece down the road before anyone found out that the car was missing.

And Jack didn't plan to linger anywhere long. He was heading north, far from Miami. The sky was clear, little traffic on the road. He reached the outskirts of St. Petersburg at false dawn and saw just what he wanted. On a deserted stretch of road stood a gas station, one of those off-brands where all they did was give you gas and oil.

He pulled in and up to the pump. A kid of eighteen or nineteen hurried out. "Fill 'er up," Jack said. "I'm goin' inside. See if you got a candy machine."

"Yes, sir, we do," the boy said. "Just about any kind of candy you crave."

We'll see if you got what I want all right, Jack thought. The glow from the fluorescent tubes in the ceiling hurt Jack's eyes. He was tired from driving nearly all night long.

There was the candy machine, just like the kid had said, but more important right there on the floor behind the desk was the safe. Jack was familiar with the sort of safe it was. He'd opened one many a time. He smiled, wondering how many times the kid had been told not to leave it standing open. Dumb kid, lucky Jack. Like stealing a baby's bottle, except there wasn't no baby around to cry. His take was just about a hundred bucks. Probably come out of the kid's salary, unless he was the owner's son or somethin'. Teach him an important lesson. Jack even got his favorite candy, a Clark Bar.

He paid the kid and took off without waiting for his change. Hell, he'd made a hundred bucks on the deal already. He pulled into the street, glanced back and saw the kid waving a couple of bills. Jack laughed. Wait till the dumb ass discovered the safe was empty.

Jack was tired but at the same time exhilarated. He was back in familiar territory now. Not his physical surroundings; he didn't know that much about Florida. But familiar in what he was doing. Fuck 'em, he thought. If they didn't want him to go straight, he damned well wouldn't.

He drove on through to Winston-Salem, North Carolina, a city he used to call home.

SEVEN

Academy life had settled into a routine. Early hours, inspections, endurance exercises, classes. After a time the discipline didn't bother Walt any more; he felt it provided a kind of security, a sameness with few surprises.

He and Roger remained best buddies, getting to know each other's ways, each other's thinking. If the chance arose, they decided, they'd get assigned to the same post, become partners.

"Sure isn't easy, is it?" Roger mused. They sat on wooden folding chairs in the recreation area waiting for a ping pong table.

"What isn't?"

"All of it. The classes, the physical conditioning."

"Nobody said it was supposed to be."

Roger laughed, Then he turned serious. "I keep worrying about Val," he said. "I shouldn't have left her when she's this far along."

"She'll be okay," Walt said.

"Thing is, she never wanted me to be a cop. My folks didn't either."

"I sure as hell can relate to that. My folks were dead set against it. Old country values. Children always obeyed their parents. Dad owns a couple of gas stations along with Avis and U-Haul franchises. Expected me to go in with him right out of high school."

"You don't have brothers and sisters?"

"Three of each."

"Couldn't your brothers help out?"

"A son is expected to work in his father's business. He offered me a partnership."

"So how'd you convince him."

"Not sure that I did."

A table opened up, and they grabbed a couple of paddles.

EIGHT

As he picked up his bag to leave the train, Bobby wondered what awaited him and Jack. It was March 20, eight months and two days since he'd been paroled and sent to Houston. Fucking assholes for sending him there. He'd wanted to go to Indiana University. If they'd sent him where he wanted to go, he wouldn't be on this trip with Twining—wherever the hell it might lead. He'd be going through the RN program. The Department of Corrections said he didn't know anyone in Indiana but he had an aunt and uncle in Houston. Who the hell could find a job in Houston, aunt and uncle notwithstanding? Nobody wanted an ex-con.

• • •

Bobby's dad was a weak man. A carpenter, trying to gouge out a living in Ponca City, Oklahoma. Trying to support a wife and three kids on the sporadic and piecemeal work handed out. Kowtowing to petty foremen and union stewards. Afraid to claim what was rightfully his. Afraid of making waves. How many times had Bobby heard his old man say: "Give thanks to the Lord for the time and a place. A time to live and a place to die. That's all any man can ask." Yeah, right. Floyd Davis most likely had heard that line in a movie and repeated it so many times he believed it himself. It was bullshit. A man could ask for a lot more!

• • •

Bobby got fair grades in school. He was smart though. Excelled in everything he cared about. Trouble was he didn't care about much. An older sister Jeanette had been good at everything, and his parents were always comparing them. They didn't seem to realize that Jeanette was six years older and naturally more advanced. Then there was Geraldine, his other sister, who died in a mental institution in Vinita, Oklahoma in 1966. She'd been hydrocephalic, and since birth had required extra attention and care. In his parents' eyes, she could do no wrong. Not so with Bobby. With him they'd been strict and unforgiving.

One night in the high school parking lot he'd pulled a knife and was charged with assault with a deadly weapon. The judge gave him two options: be sent to a reformatory or join the service.

Although it meant leaving school in his senior year and, of course, quitting the wrestling team, he'd joined the Marines. Been really "gung ho," one of the sharpest guys in boot camp at Pendleton. Once he found out how chicken shit the Corps was, he started going over the hill. Assigned to Okinawa, he was still a private when most of the guys in his outfit were wearing stripes. One night on guard duty he'd seen someone climbing the fence surrounding the dispersal office to which he'd been asked to give special attention. He called for the offender to halt. Instead, the man jumped the fence and ran. Bobby pulled out his .45 automatic, took aim and fired. At nineteen years of age, he had taken another man's life.

Marine authorities cleared him of wrongdoing. His fellow Marines did not. Sure the dead man's buddies were hatching plots of retribution, he typed a set of false orders and boarded a ship to Japan. Two weeks later he was caught trying to get onto a military base to use the PX. The result was six months in the brig, then back to the U.S. After a two-week leave in San Francisco, he was supposed to return to Camp Pendleton. That had been eight years ago.

He wasn't weak now. He and Jack Twining were strong. Tough. Coming back to make that big score.

NINE

When Walt and Roger walked into the rec area, the TV set was blaring. "From the great state of Massachusetts," a voice boomed through a tinny sound system, "may I...."

"What's going on?" Roger asked.

"Democratic Convention in Chicago. I hear they're expecting protestors."

The voice was interrupted by an on-the-spot announcer. "The auditorium is like a circus. Hippies, Yippies, and other fringe groups all wanting to be heard."

The camera switched to a shot of policemen wielding billy clubs in obviously unrestrained ferocity as they forced their way through crowds of long-haired demonstrators.

Walt nudged Roger's arm. "Be thankful we're on the CHP and not a city police department." He stared hard at the screen. "Look at these guys." A number of protesters pummeled the police with anything from fists to rocks. "There's no chance we'd ever get into something like that."

Roger turned from the screen. "You know it's happened already."

"What has?"

"The Watts riots."

Walt nodded. He'd been a senior in high school during the bloody eight days. Massive rioting supposedly touched off by two CHP officers arresting a man for drunk driving.

"And that's just the tip of the iceberg. There's UC Berkeley and...."

"Isolated cases, Rog."

"What about Oakland? The Army induction center?"

"Let's get out of here," Walt suggested. "I've had about as much as I can take."

They stood on the steps in front of the building. The night was clear, a thousand stars sparkling in an unclouded sky.

"It's a no-win situation," Roger said. "You either stand by and do nothing—for which you're blamed—or you wade in there and try to stop them. But if you do that, public sympathy is going to shift. Maybe not right away, but after a time. It happened with Watts. It happened at Berkeley. I'm not saying the protestors don't have a point...."

"Yeah, I know. Charges of police brutality. Everyone sympathizing with the Yippies, the hippies, the SDS, even the radical Weathermen. Poor defenseless victims. Nobody remembers the damaged property, the ruined buildings, the attempted killings." He expelled a sharp breath.

"I'm telling you, Rog, it's not likely we'll ever be involved in that kind of thing. You remember these cases because they're unusual."

"What are you, Walt, the eternal optimist, your glass half full no matter what?"

"You telling me that yours is half empty? Funny, I never figured you that sort of person."

"I'm not, man."

"Admit what I said is true then. We're the White Knights of the Highway. Triple-A with guns."

Roger shook his head. "You gotta face facts."

"I appreciate that you're concerned. And sure there's an off-chance we'll have to face some confrontations." He grinned. "Besides those over speeding tickets, I mean."

"Guess we won't convince each other."

"That's what makes life interesting, pal. Different ways of looking at things."

TEN

The message was clear. When people mess with the CHP, they come out second best.

Roger suspected that many of the anecdotes the cadets heard in class were exaggerations. Still, they often did appear in written reports. Officers pulling motorists over for minor traffic violations and discovering they'd committed armed robbery, kidnapping, or murder. In instance after instance, the officers won out.

Still, in the Academy entryway hung a plaque with bronze tabs listing each officer killed in the line of duty. Below appeared wording from the patrolman's oath of allegiance: "...and if necessary, lay down my life rather than swerve from the path of duty...."

Each time he glanced at the plaque Roger felt a chill. The men whose names appeared there had been alive. They'd had families and bills and mundane worries. They'd had feelings. All had gone through training and had probably stood with a lump in their throats in front of this very plaque. Now they were dead, 130 of them.

"Don't worry," Walt said coming up to stand beside him "Didn't I tell you we're gonna be stop sign jockeys. We'll work together, you and me. Nobody'll be able to touch us."

"Those guys weren't so different from you and me."

"That's true," Walt conceded. "But they're the exceptions. People die in all sorts of ways—falling down steps, getting hit by cars. You don't worry about that, do you?" Roger shook his head. "Besides," Walt continued, "no one's going to get the better of you. You're the best shot in the whole class."

Yeah, he was, Roger thought. So far, Roger had fired a perfect score on the combat firing course and shot a 290 out of 300 on the bull's eye targets. Yet he knew that shooting at a paper silhouette was not the same as the real thing. And paper targets didn't shoot back.

ELEVEN

On October 29, an officer came to the classroom and called Roger outside. "Your wife's leaving for the hospital. Labor pains are seven minutes apart." Walt loaned Roger his car.

Val was in the delivery room when Roger arrived. He wondered if Val's folks or his had been notified. There was a pay phone.

"Mrs. Gibbons?" he said when Val's mother answered.

"Roger? Is anything wrong?"

"Val's in the delivery room."

"Oh, my goodness, I'll get Dad, and we'll be right there."

Next Roger called his parents. They promised to be there too. He sat in one of the chairs and picked up a magazine. After turning page after page, he finally realized he didn't even know what the magazine was. He looked at the cover. A two-year old issue of *Sports Illustrated*. He tossed it on the end table.

Wow, he thought, how could anyone stand the waiting? He thought about Val and began to worry. Would she be okay? People did occasionally die in childbirth. God, if anything ever happened to her...

That was dumb, he told himself. Nothing was going to happen. She'd be fine and so would the baby. He walked to a window overlooking the grounds. The grass was green, the lawn well-kept. When was somebody going to tell him what was going on back there?

He sat back down, picked up the same magazine, and tried to read an article about motocross racing. He didn't care about motocross racing. He slammed the magazine down in disgust. Where were his mom and dad? His older sister? Would his brother Timmy come along? Probably not. He was seventeen. What seventeen-year-old would want to spend time hanging around the maternity ward? What about his in-laws?

After what seemed an interminable time, a nurse came toward him. "Mr. Gore?"

"Yes." His hands felt clammy cold, yet the air was stuffy.

"Your wife's fine, and so is the baby."

"What is it? A boy or...."

"I'll let your wife tell you the details."

She went on down the hall. In a moment Roger saw the double doors open and an orderly pushing a gurney. On it lay Valerie and the tiniest baby Roger had ever seen.

"Are you okay, Val? Is everything all right?"

"It's a little girl, honey. And she's perfect. Don't you think she's perfect?"

Roger looked more closely. He saw small wrinkled hands trying to make fists, red arms pulling at the air. Was she reaching for him? Could he hold her?

"Afraid you can't hold her yet," the aide said.

"Isn't she beautiful?" Val said.

"Yes," Roger whispered. How could he ever have wished for a boy? She *was* perfect! Val was perfect! Theirs had been a perfect marriage right from the start. And now it was going to be even more perfect!

The aide wheeled the gurney down the hall to a semiprivate room. Roger followed along. In a moment a nurse came in. "You can stay a few minutes," she said, "but your wife is tired. You need to give her some time to rest."

"Sure," Roger said, sitting in the chrome and plastic chair by the bed. "You're really okay?" he asked.

"I was afraid you wouldn't make it in time."

"Wouldn't miss it for anything." He told her he was going out to the waiting room. "Mom and Dad and your folks will be here."

Already Val's eyes were starting to close.

"I love you," he said as he stood. He leaned over and kissed her cheek.

"I love you."

TWELVE

It was mid-January, 1967, a relatively clear night, a respite from the tule fog. A halo encircled the moon. Roger and his friend Jimmy were cruising Main looking for girls.

Roger was attending Merced Junior College during the day, driving a school bus mornings and late afternoons and spending the evenings studying.

Tonight was different. It was a couple of weeks after Christmas, between terms at the college. Roger felt free, unencumbered. He was young, just leaving his teen years. He was driving an El Camino, sky blue, that he'd picked up for almost nothing. It needed some body work, but the motor was fine.

He pulled up to a traffic light alongside a two-tone '57 Buick, the body creamy tan, the roof near-chocolate brown.

"Will you look at that?" Jimmy said. He was a slight kid, red-haired, forehead and cheeks sprinkled with freckles. Both Jimmy and Roger wore flannel shirts, Christmas gifts from their moms and dads, and jeans beginning to define their owner's knees and groins. It was cold for Merced, down near freezing.

Roger glanced over. In the Buick were two girls. Late teens, maybe, or early twenties. "Roll down your window. Ask if they'll to meet us at the drive-in down West 14th."

"You think they'd go for that?"

"Can't hurt to try."

She was gorgeous, Roger thought, the one in the passenger seat. He'd never seen her around before and wondered if she lived in town. "Come on, Jimmy, ask 'em."

Jimmy rolled down the window and motioned for the driver of the Buick to do the same.

"So tell 'em already!"

"My buddy and I are headed for Dog 'N' Suds on West 14th. Know where it is?"

The girl laughed. She had soft blonde hair just touching her shoulders. "Not only don't know *where* it is. I don't know *what* it is."

"Drive-in restaurant. They got the best fries and root beer in town."

She turned to the girl beside her. "What do you think?" The other girl shrugged. "We'll do it," the first one said.

"Follow me," Roger called.

As the light changed, he pulled ahead and in front of the Buick. "Do you believe this?" Jimmy asked.

Roger grinned as he signaled for a right turn. In the Dog 'N' Suds lot he found two spots together.

"Looks like they're going to do it," Jimmy said.

Roger and Jimmy climbed out of the El Camino and hurried toward the Buick. A carhop came toward them, a girl named Sal whom Roger had known in high school. "So what's it gonna be?"

He turned to the two girls who were getting out of their car. "What'll you have? My treat."

The brunette smiled. "A root beer."

"Medium, large, or jumbo?"

"Small."

"We haven't got small." Sal winked. "I'm supposed to say that. So, one medium root beer."

"Come on," Jimmy said. "Live it up. Order a large."

The brunette laughed. "Small...uh, that is, medium, will be fine."

"Nothing else?" Roger asked.

"That's it."

"And you?" He turned to the blonde.

"A malted. You have malteds, right?"

"Do we ever," Sal said.

"That's all you girls want?" Jimmy said. "My buddy here's paying. Doesn't happen but once in a blue moon. Might as well enjoy. For myself, I'm going to have the tenderloin platter with cheese on the tenderloin. Great meal, right, Roger?"

"Hey, I offered to treat the girls."

"Aw, shucks, I might have known. In that case, an order of fries and a large suds."

"Same for me," Roger said.

Sal wrote the orders and left.

"So where you girls from?" Roger asked.

"Why don't we all sit down?" Jimmy pointed to a picnic table to the right of the order window.

"Good idea," Roger said.

"Lay on, Macduff," Jimmy said.

"What?" Roger asked.

"It's a line from Shakespeare," the blonde said. "*Macbeth*. Didn't you read that in high school? Sophomore English?"

"Who remembers sophomore English?" Roger sat on one of the benches. The girls took seats on the other side.

"Big college man now, right?" Jimmy said. "Merced Junior College. Gonna be a cop. Always wanted to be a cop, my buddy here. Practically worshipped cops from the time he was a little tad on his mama's knee."

"Enough!" Roger said, embarrassed. He turned to the girls. "I'm Roger. Roger Gore, and this is...."

"Jimmy Fontana," Jimmy said. "And you're..." He stared at the blonde. "April."

Roger looked directly into the brunette's eyes. "What's your name?"

"Valerie. Everyone calls me Val."

"You live here in town?" Jimmy asked.

"I do," April said. "And Val's my cousin. She lives in...."

Val interrupted. "In Phoenix."

"You're visiting?" Roger asked.

"For a couple of days. I go home tomorrow morning."

"Just my luck."

Val laughed, half mockingly, half in regret. "Sorry, Roger, but that's the way it goes."

Sal came up to them carrying a tray of drinks and fries. "I take it you're staying here," Sal said.

"Don't I wish," Roger mumbled.

"I mean you're not going back to your cars!"

"Oh, yeah, right." Roger pulled a fiver from his pocket and handed it to Sal. She took the drinks and fries from the tray and placed them on the table, then counted out the change.

"Hey, Val," Roger said, "sure you won't have some fries?"

"Maybe one or two." Gingerly, she pulled one from the bag on the table.

"April?" Jimmy held out his bag to her. She shook her head.

"You're going to be a cop?" Val asked.

"Taking law enforcement classes anyhow."

"Don't let him kid you," Jimmy said. "He's never wanted to be anything else but a cop."

"You're here just till tomorrow?" Roger asked.

"'Fraid so," Val answered. "Then back to the salt mines."

"Work? School?"

"Secretary."

"But you're from Merced?" Jimmy asked April.

"Born and raised. Live on the East side of town."

"Probably why I've never seen you." Jimmy hesitated. "Look, I realize you don't know me. But do you think..."

"Yes?" April asked.

"Do you think I might have your phone number?"

"You're right," April said. "I don't know you."

"I'm not a serial killer. I don't kick dogs or beat up old ladies."

"You're a riot," April said, her voice showing he was far less than a riot.

"Gee, thanks. I think you're a riot too."

April laughed. "Is that so?"

"So anyhow," Jimmy said, "can I have your phone number? I live here in town. Just like you. Born and raised."

April turned to Val. "What do you think? Should I give it to him?"

"He seems all right."

"You've worn me down." She gave him the number as Roger focused on Val.

"No chance of staying any longer, I suppose. No chance.... Forget it." Roger looked up to see Val staring at him, a puzzled look on her face. Or maybe a look of indecision.

"So anything you girls would like to do? Go to a movie, maybe. I hear there's an old Gene Autry...."

"Gene Autry!" Jimmy said.

"Hey, what's wrong with Gene Autry? In my opinion, he's the one should be king of the cowboys. Not an upstart like that Rogers guy."

Val and April giggled.

"We have to get back," Val said. "All that packing."

Roger noticed a look pass between April and Val.

"Sure, I understand."

"If things were only different...," Val said.

"It's all right." He crumpled up the empty bags and stuffed them into a root beer mug. "I suppose we'd better be going."

"I'll call you," Jimmy told April, who looked at him and shrugged.

Roger and Jimmy watched the two girls climb back into the Buick and pull out onto the street.

"Got it bad, don't you?"

"I've never felt this way before," Roger answered. "Never wanted to be with any girl so much before. Man, I don't even know her last name."

"Like I said, you got it bad."

"At least you have a phone number for April."

"Some of us got it and some of us don't."

Roger grinned as he reached over and punched Jimmy lightly on his upper arm.

Roger couldn't get Valerie out of his mind. In class, her vision would intrude on the lecture. When he was driving to work or home from class, he saw her face in passing cars. "Gotta get hold of yourself, young fella," he told himself half mockingly as he drove home one day. "Phoenix is not next door." But it wasn't all that far either, was it? A few hundred miles. Maybe he could find out her number. Maybe they at least could talk on the phone.

It suddenly occurred to him. Jimmy had April's number. April was Valerie's cousin.

He pulled into the carport of his parents house and hurried inside. "Hi, Mom," he said as he rushed to the phone. His mom was in the alcove off the kitchen.

"Hi, Roger. How was...."

"Talk to you later!" He hurried into the living room, picked up the phone and dialed Jimmy's number. He heard the phone ring twice, three times.

"Hello."

"Will you give me April's number?"

"Hey, slow down here. I thought you were interested in...."

"Val! Yeah. That's why I want April's number."

"You gonna call Arizona, man?"

"Will you give me the number?"

"No problem. But first the little matter of that bag of fries and the mug of root beer I owe you for."

Roger laughed. "All right, we're all squared away."

He hung up and immediately dialed April's home. An older woman answered.

"May I speak to April, please?"

"Who is it?"

"Roger. I'm...."

"Yes, I'm April's grandma. She told me how much you were taken by her cousin. Just a moment." Roger heard the phone being laid down and in a moment picked up again.

"Roger?"

"You told your grandma about me?"

"You really like Val, huh?"

"Will you give me her number? I'd like to call..."

"I can't."

"Why not?"

"I'm sorry."

"Didn't she like me or what?"

"She liked you. A lot. At least that's what she told me."

"So what's the problem?"

"The problem is she was stuck with telling you.... I can't say anything more."

"I know the whole thing's not practical. I'm in school, working part-time. She's off in Arizona."

"She's not in Arizona."

"What?"

"I said...she's not in Arizona."

"I don't follow."

"She just said that...so she wouldn't be annoyed."

"I see."

"No, you don't see." Roger heard a sigh on the other end of the line. "She likes you too." There was a pause. "I've gone this far. I might as well tell you the rest. She lives in La Grand."

"La Grand. But that's about twenty miles—"

"Exactly. Her father's constable there."

"You're kidding. My dad was a constable in Snelling." He took a deep breath. "Why did she tell me she lived in Phoenix?"

"She was on vacation there. Just got back. She thought it would be fun to see if she could pull it off."

"I guess she really got me, huh?"

"She does like you, Roger."

"Sure seems like it."

"She was just being silly...at first. She told me later she wished she hadn't done it. She said you seem like a really nice person."

"So where does that leave me?"

"Tell you what. Maybe she'll kill me, but I'm going to risk it. You got a pencil?"

"A pen, yeah."

"Then here's her number."

"Thanks, April. You don't know how much—"

"I suppose you'll have to admit I told you."

"I'll tell her I wore you down."

He hung up and once more picked up the phone.

"Valerie?"

"Who's this?"

"Roger. Roger Gore. We met last week at the drive-in. Well, not exactly at the—"

"Roger!" Her voice sounded incredulous. "How did you find out where I live?"

"Told you I was going to be a cop, didn't I? Told you I was taking law enforcement classes."

Her laugh was genuine. Roger started to laugh as well.

"So you called me, huh?"

"Would you...would you consider going to that movie? I mean it doesn't have to be Gene Autry—"

"When?"

Roger chuckled. "I'd ask you for tonight, but I realize that's pretty short notice. Anyhow, I gotta study. Got a quiz coming up. How about Friday evening?"

"I accept."

"We could get something to eat, and— You accept?"

"About 6:30, is that okay? It'll take awhile to get back to Merced. Or would you rather I meet you in town? I really am a secretary."

"I'll come pick you up. Just give me directions."

Thirteen

The fog was thick, already making visibility almost nil. It was the middle of March, and Roger and Val were going to a dance at the junior college. A big deal, and he didn't want to disappoint her.

He hit a cow. A Jersey cow right in the middle of the road. He killed it, pretty much totaled his car, and got pretty well bruised and battered. So instead of the dance, he went to the hospital. For observation, to see if he'd had a concussion. He felt pretty silly.

Jimmy arranged to have Roger's car towed back to Merced. Roger asked him to call Valerie and tell her what had happened. Just before visiting hours ended she rushed into the room and up to the bed.

"Oh, God," she said, "I'm sorry. If you hadn't been coming to pick me up—"

"Are you trying to blame yourself for what happened?"

"I could look out the window, see how foggy it was. I could have called you."

"It's my own darn fault. A cow! Can you believe it!"

"Just so you're okay."

"I'm fine."

"You're sure."

"I'm going to go home tomorrow morning."

"Roger, if anything happened to you... And to think how close we came to never seeing each other again."

"It wasn't anything serious. For me, I mean. For the cow, it was different."

"I mean telling you I lived in Phoenix."

"Will you marry me?"

"What?"

"Will you marry me?" He chuckled. "I'm not exactly in a position to get down on my knees."

Valerie broke out laughing, and the laughter turned to tears. "I mean it. I don't know what I'd do if I'd lose you."

"Marry me, and you won't. What do you say?"

"Of course, I'll marry you."

"When do you want this to happen?"

"What?"

"The sooner the better. You told me your dad was a constable. Well, mine was too. That means the marriage was fated to be."

"You're crazy, you know?"

"Let's set the date."

"There are so many things to plan. First, we have to tell Mom and Dad. And your folks."

"It'll all work out."

FOURTEEN

Roger tried to tell his folks he and Val were getting married.

"You're too young," his dad said.

"Lots of guys my age—"

"And most of them end up divorced."

"My God, we aren't even married yet."

"And so far as I'm concerned, you won't be."

"That's your final word."

"That's my final word, Roger. Your mother's too."

"Is that right, Mom?"

"Roger, you're still a baby."

"Mom, I'm twenty years old. How old were you when you married Dad?"

"It was a different time," Max said. "A totally different set of circumstances."

"That's all you can say?"

"I'm sorry," Max said. "But you have your whole life before you. You need to finish school, get a good-paying job."

"I don't believe this."

"I'm sorry."

Roger turned and stormed from the house. Things weren't going so well for Valerie either, or so she told him later.

For a time he walked through the neighborhood aimlessly, up and down familiar streets. At a drugstore on the corner was a phone booth. Roger checked his pocket for change. Just about enough. He hurried into the booth and closed the door.

• • •

Valerie agreed. The only thing they could do was elope. Roger went back to his room, packed a few belongings in an old leather suitcase and started to take it outside.

"Where do you think you're going?" Max asked.

"None of your business."

"It's my business all right if you take my car."

"Okay, damn it. Val and I are going to Reno."

"Reno!" his dad stormed. "What do you mean by doing that?"

"Seems everyone is against our marriage. We're going to take it into our own hands."

"Absolutely not!" Max said rushing toward the door.

"We'll see," Roger said skirting around him and on outside.

Roger hurried to the car, threw in his suitcase and headed out toward La Grand. Valerie stood waiting on the porch.

"Hi, Val," Roger said. "Listen, if you're not sure we're doing the right thing..."

"Come on, let's get going before Mom and Dad get home. I left them a note."

"Where are they?"

"Grocery shopping."

"You didn't talk to them?"

She tossed her things into the back and scooted in beside him. Since his car was still in the garage, he'd taken the Plymouth. Mom still had her car, so it wouldn't be a problem. She rarely used it anyhow, and Dad could drive it. "Let's just go."

Roger leaned over and kissed her cheek. "I love you, too." He backed out of the driveway and headed north toward Sacramento.

"I do love you, Roger, or I wouldn't be doing this."

"I know that." He gave her a quick glance and a smile.

Somewhere between Donner Pass and the Nevada border, Roger heard a siren. He glanced into the rearview mirror to see red spotlights on top of a black-and-white. The CHP. He was puzzled. He hadn't done anything wrong. He was driving well within the speed limit, paying attention to the road.

He pulled over to the side.

"What is it?" Val asked.

Roger shook his head.

He glanced in the mirror to see the officer checking his dad's license plates. Hand resting on the butt of his revolver, he cautiously approached. Standing a few feet away, he motioned for Roger to open the door.

"What is it, officer?" Roger asked.

"Get out, please. Don't make any sudden moves. You too, miss."

"What's wrong?" Val asked. Roger could see she was frightened, her hands shaking.

"Just please do as I say." The officer was about forty. Roger stepped out and stood by the car. Val slid under the steering wheel and got out to stand beside him.

"Where are you two headed?" the officer asked.

"To Reno, why?" Roger asked.

"May I see your license?"

Roger reached around to his back pocket and removed his wallet. Since the man seemed wary, Roger made his movements slow and deliberate. He opened the wallet, pulled out his license, and extended it. The officer took it and studied it.

"You're Roger Gore?"

"That's right."

"Your name, miss?"

"Valerie Gibbons."

"Where are you two coming from?"

"Merced. That's where I live," Roger said. "Val's from La Grand. That's where I picked her up."

"What's the purpose of this trip?"

Roger smiled and glanced at Val. "We're going to get married, that is, as soon as we find a judge or a preacher."

"Eloping, is that it?" Roger noticed a slight smile on the officer's face.

"Yes, sir. Neither Val's parents nor mine particularly approve. I mean, it isn't that they disapprove. They just want us to wait."

"Hang on just a moment, will you please?"

He and Val stood by the car as the officer got into his black-and-white and talked to someone on his radio. In a minute or so he was back.

"Everything all right?" Roger asked.

"Thank you." He handed back Roger's license. "You can be on your way." His eyes twinkled. "Congratulations and best wishes. You folks take care now. Drive safely." He nodded and headed back to the cruiser. Then he turned. "Once you get to Reno and get things taken care of, it might be a good idea if you'd call both sets of parents and tell them your whereabouts."

"Sure thing," Roger answered as the man turned and headed back to his car.

"Wonder what that was all about," Val said as they climbed back inside.

"You got me," Roger said. "He certainly acted like something was up."

"You suppose he was looking for someone? Maybe with a car like this."

"Maybe. But the way he checked the license plate... I don't know."

Roger pulled back onto the highway. In Reno, he and Val found that their troubles still weren't over. Nobody would marry them. Val was nineteen, and that was okay. According to Nevada law, a woman could marry at eighteen, but a man needed to be twenty-one or have parental consent.

They kept trying "I'm sure getting sick of seeing that doggone river," Val said. The Truckee River ran through downtown Reno, and Roger knew they must have crossed it four or five times in their search.

"Everybody seems to know our story here," Val said. "And we seem to be out of luck."

"Want to try Carson City?"

"What?"

"It's smaller, maybe less sophisticated."

"What are you thinking?" Val asked.

"Well, you see on the way here we stopped overnight at a motel up in Reno. Separate rooms, of course. It was late; we were with friends. As a sort of prank, two or three of them picked me up and threw me into the swimming pool. Darned if it didn't ruin my ID. Driver's license, birth certificate, everything. And you know what? I was so upset I didn't have the presence of mind to try to dry them out."

Val threw back her head and laughed. "You think it'll work?"

"We won't know till we try."

The minister was a little skeptical, but he did go along with it. As soon as they were married and had rented a motel room, Val called her mother.

"Why'd you go and do this, Val?"

"You know why, Mom. We didn't want to wait. You wanted us to. Roger's folks were adamant about it.

"I just wish you hadn't—"

"I know, Mom. But it's done. I'm Mrs. Roger Gore."

"Oh, honey, this isn't what I dreamed of."

"Will you wish us good luck?"

"You know I will. I love you. You tell Roger... You tell him I love him too."

Next Roger called his folks. His father answered the phone. "Dad, it's—" The receiver slammed down. He turned to Val. "It was Dad. He hung up."

"They'll come around."

"You don't know my old man."

When they arrived back in Merced, Roger drove by the garage where his car was to have been repaired. It was ready. He drove the Plymouth while Val followed him back to his house driving his car.

He pulled into the driveway feeling apprehensive, hating to face his mom and dad. He stopped the car, went up and decided he'd better knock rather than walk right in.

"Who is it?" It was his mother.

"It's me, Mom."

"I don't think we want to see you just now."

"I didn't do anything horrible."

"You heard your mother," Max called. "I think you'd better leave."

"I brought back your keys." He waited for an answer. When none came, he dropped the keys in the mailbox and headed out to the El Camino.

"I saw what happened," Val said.

"You want to drive?"

"Where are we going?"

"House hunting," he said.

"House hunting?"

"House or apartment, I don't care which."

They found a house a few blocks from Roger's parents. Val insisted he call and tell them where he and Val were. When his mother answered, he blurted out the address before she could hang up. Val called her folks who invited her and Roger to Sunday dinner.

"At least someone's being civil," Roger said.

Roger tried to call several times and finally gave up. Three weeks later, there was a knock on the door. It was his mother and father, loaded down with groceries.

It wasn't till a couple of months later that Roger found out why the CHP officer had stopped him and Val. Max had reported his Plymouth stolen.

FIFTEEN

Walt had enrolled at Merced Junior College with the idea of getting a degree in law enforcement and later joining the FBI. Then he discovered they wanted only lawyers or accountants. That wasn't what Walt had in mind. He didn't want to sit in an office going over business accounts. He didn't want to be involved in litigation. He wanted to be out on the job, going after the bad guys.

The day he found out he came home from class and told Nicki.

"So what are you going to do?" she asked. She handed him a cup of coffee and sat across from him at the kitchen table.

"Not sure," Walt said. "Except I've been thinking..."

"What?"

"Of applying to the CHP?"

"The Highway Patrol?"

"Why not?" They were as different as the two sides of the moon, Walt thought, Nicki red-haired and noisy, he dark and quiet. People often asked how they ended up together. She preferred boisterous parties; he liked quiet evenings with her and the kids.

"Why the CHP?" Nicki asked.

"Because they're the best, I suppose."

She looked into his eyes. "Why do you want to be a cop?"

"I don't know. My way of making the world right, maybe."

"You want everyone calling you pig? That's what you'll get. People our age. Hippies."

"What do I care what hippies do?"

"I'm just saying—"

"Saying what?" He hated to argue. He wanted to place his hand on hers, to reassure her. But this was too important.

"Why do you want to be a policeman?"

"I'm taking law enforcement, Nicki, not psychology. Do I want to feel big? Do I want to feel important? Is that what you're asking?"

"I don't mean to get you upset. I just think you need to examine—"

"I don't get this. You thought it was okay that I wanted to join the FBI. Didn't you think that?"

"You want the truth? I'll tell you the truth. No, it wasn't okay. Do you think I want to worry each day? Every time you go to work? Do you think I'd like to spend my life scared?"

"Scared?"

"That you won't come home. That you'll be— God, Walt!"

"If that's what's worrying you—"

"That's what's worrying me."

"The CHP. They don't fight big-time crooks or gangsters. They give out traffic tickets."

"I suppose."

She paused and took a breath. "You really want to do this?"

"More than anything."

"I don't like it. Not knowing where you are, if you're okay."

"I told you—"

"I know what you— I know. The CHP writes traffic tickets."

He laughed. "That really is what they do."

"Okay."

"What do you mean, okay?"

"I mean... I guess if it's what you want, I won't stand in your way."

Walt leaned over and kissed her cheek. "I love you, Nicki Frago."

She cuddled against him.

"So all we have to do now," he said, "is convince my mom and dad." And that, Walt thought, was going to be some battle.

SIXTEEN

At the time Roger was told to report to the Academy, Val became pregnant. He felt he should waive the offer for the time being.

"It makes more sense that way," he told her.

"You've looked forward to the Academy too long," she answered.

"I'll wait till next year." It was Friday evening just after work. They sat on the Danish modern couch, a relic dug from an aunt's garage.

"If you wait, you'll resent it."

"Now just hold on!" he said.

"I'm suggesting that you have a chance now. You made it through everything. The background investigation." She peered intently into his eyes. "Didn't you tell me it's hard to get past that?" She waited. "It's not going to get easier later?"

"Once the baby is a little older—"

"There'll be expenses. Maybe a second child. We'll want a bigger place...."

"But the baby's due in—"

"I'm going to miss you."

"I'll have weekends free. Saturday noon to Sunday night."

SEVENTEEN

More than halfway through the training Walt still hadn't lost a bluey. He wondered if this would help him in getting the assignment he wanted or maybe later in being promoted.

In the chow line he struck up a conversation with an officer back for in-service training. The four hash marks on his sleeve told Walt he'd been on the job twenty plus years.

"I'm curious, sir. What was done about discipline back in the 40s?"

"Discipline?"

"Blueys. Did you have them then?"

The man chuckled. "Did we ever. I was married back then. You married?"

"Yes, sir. I have two children."

"I had a son. College instructor now. Physics. UC Davis."

"Girl and a boy, one and two."

"Bet you're proud as punch, eh? I know I was. So being married, I was determined not to be restricted to grounds. Got my fifth bluey the week of graduation. Then, of course, it didn't matter. How about you?"

"So far I've been lucky."

"You have all your blueys! Incredible."

"I was wondering... If I make it through without getting any gigs, do you think it'll help?"

"Help?"

"When I'm out in the field?"

The man guffawed. "Oh yeah! It'll help all right. The Academy will tell your captain all about it so he can warn everyone of the weird duck coming in. Bet you're the type of guy who volunteered to clean the blackboard in fourth grade too."

Walt felt the blood rush to his face. A couple of instructors stood nearby. All of them broke into laughter. Nearby cadets gave Walt strange looks. He chose a seat by himself and didn't look up for the rest of the meal.

The following morning during reveille inspection, the commander stopped in front of Walt. "Where's your tie clasp, cadet?" he asked.

"I'm not wearing it, sir," Walt answered.

"So I see. I'm going to ask you to hand over one of your blueys. Next time maybe you'll remember to wear the proper uniform."

Walt smiled to himself. Yes, sir, the next time he would remember. There was no doubt about it.

EIGHTEEN

"So tell me about the baby," Walt said.

"A girl. We named her Janine. Janine Gore."

"I remember our first. How Nicki and I looked forward to the birth. Must have been bad for Val, your being here."

"I hated to leave. Val's mom's going to stay a few days. You know..."

"Yeah?"

"I thought all new babies had faces like prunes."

"Janine didn't, I suppose," Walt kidded.

"She's beautiful, Walt. The most beautiful girl in the world."

"Not that you're prejudiced or anything."

"Of course not.... I can't wait to be done. To spend time with her. I hate to miss these first few weeks."

"You have weekends."

"It's not the same. I don't want to miss a single minute of her growing up."

"I know. Even when they scream all night with colic, I wouldn't trade them."

NINETEEN

The class was queried on their choice of assignments. Most openings were in the Los Angeles basin, with a few in the Bay Area and one or two in the desert. Each cadet listed choices from most to least desirable. As Roger remarked, "How do you determine the most desirable from a string of undesirables?"

Selections were arbitrary, with property owners and those with children in school getting a slight edge.

Roger and Walt had weighed each possibility. Neither could visualize assignment to such remote desert locales as Blythe or Banning. Los Angeles had too much traffic and smog, leaving only the Bay Area.

"What do you think?" Walt asked.

"Well, I've never been there," Roger said, "but Redwood City sounds nice."

"How about Oakland second?" Walt said. "The Raiders are going great guns!."

The two agreed that after that would come San Francisco, Hayward and Concord, followed by a number of areas in and around Los Angeles.

Two days later, the assignments were posted. Walt lost sight of Roger as he pushed his way forward in the jostling mob, but he heard him yelling a short time later.

"Hey Walt! We got it, man. We're going to be partners!"

"Where?"

"L. A.! We're going together."

"Will you slow down and tell me where!"

"West Valley. That's in Van Nuys and Hollywood."

"Hollywood! Great! Let's call the girls and tell them."

"Hold on. There's one thing I didn't tell you—West Valley's a new office. Not built yet. In the meantime, we go to Newhall."

"Newhall? Where in the hell is that?"

"I'm not sure. Down that way somewhere, I guess. But no sweat, we're going together!"

"Newhall," Walt muttered. He wondered what kind of place it was.

TWENTY

When he reached Winston-Salem, Jack was exhausted but at the same time exhilarated. The 600-mile drive had worn him down, but he knew he couldn't sleep. Couldn't even think about sleeping. So he might as well check things out. He figured the damned world owed him. Until he was repaid, he'd take what was his.

He'd meant to go straight. But the fucking feds wouldn't let him. Up ahead was a building supply store. Didn't look like they had much security. Lights dim around the entrance. No lights at the side and back. A dim bulb burning above the cash register. He still had money from his job in Miami. But what the shit, he could always use more. It was getting on toward morning when he pulled up to the curb and locked the car. Didn't want anyone stealing it now, did he?

At the first hotel he came to, decrepit-looking but clean, he booked a room for the night. Almost before his head touched the pillow, he was out.

The next night he hit the building supply store—net of a thousand bucks—a dry cleaners and a Kentucky Fried Chicken, the latter two for about enough money to buy a train ticket out to the West Coast. He went back to the hotel, slept till morning, got up, showered and shaved, collected his things and went outside. He hailed a taxi and told the driver to take him to the train station. He bought a ticket, got himself a Coke and a candy bar and sat on a bench to wait. He was going to go fishing again, this time out in Seattle.

TWENTY-ONE

It was only late August, but Jack shivered as he stepped off the train. Christ, it was cold and dismal; he knew right away he'd made a mistake. First thing was to get some warmer clothes.

Once he was settled into a rooming house, he decided to look for a job. Dark clouds hovered over the bleak coastline and washed out buildings. It reminded him of Alcatraz, and he shivered again, this time not so much from the cold. He stopped for a cup of coffee, clutching the hot mug in both hands.

At a nearby booth sat a man his age. "Gonna be a long damned winter, you ask me," the man said making conversation. He pushed away a plate of congealed egg yellow and toast crumbs.

"Oh, yeah?" Jack said. "I just got in. Weather been like this for a while?"

"Damned Alaska current. Colder than usual." He nodded out the window toward the sea. "Water gets choppy like this, you know you're in for it."

"Thought I might get me a job," Jack said. "Fishing."

The man was big-boned and blond. "Got any experience? If you ain't got experience, you might as well forget it."

"Yeah," Jack said, pulling a cigarette from the pack in his shirt pocket. "Worked on a fishing boat out of Miami." He put the Chesterfield between his lips and pulled out his Zippo. He lit the cigarette, his first of the day. He inhaled deeply before going on. "Decided I needed a change of scenery. Never been to the West Coast before."

"You belong to the Union?"

"Naw."

"I wish you luck then. You're going to need it."

"How's that?" Jack asked.

"Union got everything wrapped up tight around here. It's one of them conundrums life likes to throw you every now and then."

"Conundrums?"

"Puzzles."

"What do you mean?" Jack flicked ashes toward the thick glass ashtray that said "Vince's Place for the Best Breakfasts in Town."

"Well, you see, to get a union job, you gotta belong to the union. At the same time you can't belong to the union till you get a union job."

"You a fisherman?" Jack asked.

"That I am."

"Know anyone's who's hiring?"

"Like I said..."

"Thanks anyhow, buddy." Jack signaled for the check. Son-of-a-bitch! he thought as he calculated a tip and got up to pay the bill. The world was still dealing him a shitload. Maybe he was wrong. What the hell was so good about going straight anyhow? Then he thought again of Alcatraz and the other federal pens where he'd done time. Fuck it all, he'd still rather be in Florida. But he'd give it a little time here and see what happened. Surely, there was some damned boat that needed a hand.

It was the same story no matter where he went. "I got a union boat, man. You don't belong to the union, I just can't hire you."

"Can you at least tell me where I might find work?" Jack always asked. He followed each lead but found it led nowhere. He took to buying the daily papers and perusing the want ads.

The longer he went without a job, the angrier he became. He realized that his attitude wasn't helping, but maybe he just didn't give a fuck. One of the men told him he might find a job in the fish sheds cleaning the catch.

Okay, he thought, maybe it was better than nothing. His money was running out. He had enough for a week yet, a couple if he stretched it.

The smell was nearly overpowering, but worse than that, nearly all the workers were women. And he wasn't about to take no women's work.

Hell, he thought, no matter how hard a man tried, if life dealt him a bad hand of cards, there wasn't much he could do. Well, maybe there was one thing. He knew this guy in Saint Louis. Name of Billy Ray Smallen. They'd served time together in Leavenworth. Hadn't seen one another since 1963 when Jack was transferred to Tallahassee, but they'd kept in touch through the prison grapevine.

Maybe Billy Ray had something going, Jack thought. Maybe the two of them could get together and score a few times. One thing was for damned sure. No more was Jack trying the straight and narrow. Fuck 'em, he thought. Every goddamned one of 'em. Just fuck 'em to hell.

Twenty-Two

Jack stepped off the train in St. Louis. He was tired, bored out of his gourd and ready for some action. First thing he was going to do was find a place to stay and then look up his buddy. They'd gotten along fine in the time they knew each other. Billy Ray'd done time for forging money orders and had been released only six, seven months back. Hell, Jack didn't know why he'd wasted the time he had out in Seattle. He could probably do a lot better right here.

He called Billy Ray, and the two of them arranged to meet. Billy Ray was a couple of years younger than Jack but a meaner son-of-a-bitch it would be hard to find anywhere. Wasn't nothing he wasn't capable of doing, Jack thought. Good thing they'd gotten along. Jack knew if it came down to it, he could take him fair and square. But then again he doubted Billy Ray would be willing to play fair and square.

Still it was good to see him sitting in the corner of the bar when Jack walked in. "Hey, buddy, how you doing?" Jack called as soon as he spied him.

"Well, Twining, you're looking good," Billy Ray said. He was an inch or two shorter than Jack but fifty pounds heavier, most of it muscle, some of it gut. His hair was red and his freckled face as speckly as a bird's egg.

"You too, man." Jack slid in opposite him and ordered a beer. When it came, he took a deep swallow. It was hot as hell in St. Louis, or maybe it only seemed that way because of the month he'd spent in Seattle.

"What's up?" Billy Ray asked.

"Looking for some action," Jack said. "Wondering if you could help me out."

"Might could do that. Let me think here a minute or two." Billy took a slug of the whiskey that had been sitting in front of him. "What are you looking for?" he asked.

"Depends on what kind of action you got."

"I hear there's a savings and loan up to Decatur."

"Illinois?"

"Where the hell else is Decatur, Jack?"

"You trying to say I'm stupid or something?"

"Cool it, man. I didn't mean—"

"Yeah? Well, how about you just telling me about this savings and loan up there in Decatur?"

"Not federally insured, so there ain't gonna be no FBI nosing around. Supposed to be a hell of an easy touch."

"If it's such an easy touch, why ain't you been there yourself?"

"Got things going for me here, man."

"Oh, yeah?"

"Look, Twining, I'm doing you a favor. You trying to call me on it or what?"

"All right, all right. I was only asking."

"Like I said, the place is an easy touch."

"No disrespect, Billy Ray, but how do you know that?"

"Place's been robbed twice in the last twelve months. Each time in the double digit thousands. Everyone knows the layout, how things are run there."

"And you're willing to provide me with all the detail?"

"We're buddies, ain't we?"

"What's the catch, Billy Ray?"

"You doubting me, Twining?"

"Ain't doubting you at all. Just saying I know you. We go way back."

Billy Ray laughed. "Okay then, here's the thing. I'll give you the address and tell you what I know for ten percent of the take."

"Sounds reasonable to me."

"So we got us a deal then?"

"If the place is as easy as you say—"

"It's easy all right. Couldn't ask for better."

"I'm going to need a gun, Billy Ray."

"That can be arranged."

"Then I guess we got us a deal."

• • •

Jack met with Billy Ray one more time before stealing a car and driving to Decatur. Billy Ray gave him a gun he said was clean—a Colt .45—and told him the best time to hit the savings and loan was just before 4 p.m. They were bound to have a lot of money on hand to cash payroll checks.

Jack stole a Chevy station wagon, dark green, and headed out toward Decatur, maybe a hundred or a hundred and twenty miles, he figured.

He hit town, found the address and drove around the block a couple of times. It did look easy. It was small, as such buildings go, and so there were few employees. He parked around the corner and let the motor run.

The savings and loan was the second building from the corner. There were two employees, a girl of nineteen or twenty in a teller's cage and a man off in a little office with a sign that read "Manager." Not even a guard. The only thing Jack had to worry about was the burglar alarm, and he figured he'd be long gone before the police responded. He'd make sure nobody could trip the alarm till he was out of the building.

Everything went according to plan. Jack pulled the Colt .45 from his waistband, pointed it at the teller who he thought was going to shit her pants and demanded she hand over whatever she had in her cash drawer. He saw there was very little cash. "What the fuck is this? I said all of it, and I do mean all."

The color disappeared from the young woman's face. "There are checks, sir" the girl said. "That's all the cash I have."

"Stuff it into a money bag now!"

"Yes, sir." She scooped up the checks and cash and shoved them into a bag.

The manager, a man in his forties in a brown business suit, apparently saw what was happening and stepped out of his office. Jack turned, the gun pointed at the man's chest. "I want you over by the lady! Get moving, and I mean fast."

The man swallowed hard and did as he was told.

"Now," Jack said, "I want cash. All you have. Not the piddling amount the bitch here tried to give me."

"Sir?" the man said.

"If you do what I say, you won't get hurt. Now give me your cash."

The man glanced at the money bag. "I'm sorry, sir. That's all we have on hand."

"I'll warn you just one more time."

"And I'm telling you, sir, we have no more cash. It's late Friday afternoon. Payday. Everyone cashing his checks."

"What!"

"Sir, we don't have any more—"

His hand shook, his gut burned. He swung the Colt .45 toward the manager's chest and fired. The impact knocked the man backward. Blood streamed from the hole in his chest. Jack fired again. Blood poured out of his chest and mouth and ears.

Jack grabbed the bag, turned and raced outside, his heart beating against his ribs like a fighting cock locked in a bird cage.

He leaped into the car and floored the accelerator, barely aware of the clanging of the bank's alarm. He hardly took his foot off the accelerator the entire way back to St. Louis. He slammed the tire against the curb in front of Billy Ray's house, grabbed the pistol from where he'd thrown it beside him and raced up the steps. He beat on the door with the butt of the gun.

"What the fuck's going on."

"Open the goddamned door."

"What the hell—"

Jack aimed the gun at Billy Ray's chest. "You dumb shit! You asshole. You fucking piece of crap!"

"Take it easy, Jack. Take it easy, man. What the hell's going on?"

"I'll tell you what's going on. Whoever told you about that savings and loan got things just a mite fucked up."

"Hey, man, stop swinging that gun and tell me what went wrong."

"There was no fucking money."

"What!"

"It was too late, Billy Ray. Payroll checks had all been cashed. So what do I get. I'd guess maybe a thousand dollars and a hell of a lot of worthless checks."

"We can work something out."

"We better work something out. Or you're dead, Billy Ray. And I don't make idle threats."

"Put the gun away. Christ, Twining, you're going to have cops swarming all over the place—"

"Get the fuck inside and shut up."

Smallen provided him with a car, a '62 Corvair. It was stolen but had cold plates. There was a forged bill of sale and ownership certificate. In return for the checks, which were worthless to Jack, Billy Ray gave him weapons—two Colt .45 automatic pistols and a .9 mm Browning automatic. The former were stamped "U.S. property" and were probably hot, but what the hell. Jack was hot as well. He'd violated parole, was an ex-con in possession of a firearm, and maybe the police didn't know it yet, but he'd robbed an S and L and shot the manager. The fact the firearms were stolen was of little consequence. The other pistol was probably stolen too, but a very nice weapon.

Jack left St. Louis and drove to Winston-Salem. Once there, he took a small furnished room, rented to him by another prison acquaintance named George Opel Payne whom Jack had served with for several months in Atlanta.

Later, lost in thought, watching his clothes tumble in a Laundromat dryer half a block from the room he'd rented, Jack was startled when a young woman asked if he'd watch her clothes while she went out to put money in the parking meter.

"Sure," Jack said, "go ahead." She was a brunette in her mid-twenties. A few moments later she was back.

"Thank you kindly," she said taking a seat a couple of chairs away. The seats were molded plastic, yellow and green. She was about five, nine, over-weight and bordering on fat. She wore a t-shirt that was stretched out of shape and jeans two sizes too big. She nodded toward the dryer. "Kind of like life, ain't it?" she said. "All that bouncing around till everything's all mixed up."

Jack laughed. "You got that right," he said.

She had a nice face, kind of heart-shaped and smooth.

"Name's Jack," he told her. "Jack Twining. Just moved in down the block."

"Dee Mauldin. I ain't been in town long neither. From Fayettsville. Got me a divorce and decided to set out on my own. Got a job waitressing at a café. Place named Toby's, over the other side of town."

His whole life he'd been alone. Emotionally and the way he lived. He sup-posed it suited him. Even in prison, he'd always maintained an aloofness. Dee gave him her number, and he decided to call.

TWENTY-THREE

Jack clung to the fact that somewhere his mother was still alive. As a kid, he'd told himself that she hadn't wanted to give him up, that if she'd had the choice she wouldn't have left him to be raised in foster homes where nobody cared how he felt. An incurable disease, he told himself. She had an incurable disease and didn't want to risk his getting it. It was traumatic and extreme, but she had nowhere else to turn. So she took her precious baby and laid him on the steps of the orphanage.

At other times Jack thought perhaps he'd been fathered by a priest and born to a Catholic nun. Forced to choose between him and the priest, she'd done the honorable thing, sacrificed her boy to save the priest's reputation and the church's.

The woman in the last foster home had slipped and told Jack she knew of his mother's whereabouts. Now that he was back, he decided to look her up. Her name was Cross, a widow or divorcee, he didn't know which.

Jack was certain that if he could find his real mother, if he could just even talk to her, either on the phone or in person, everything would be better. His life would be better. That's all it would take to turn things around. Often he visualized her, a woman probably now in her fifties. A shadowy figure, attractive, strong. He could never visualize a face.

Fifteen years since he'd seen Mrs. Cross. Still he remembered the house on Olive—old, two-story with a railing around the front porch. It seemed smaller, run down and in need of paint. He parked, walked up on the porch and knocked.

The woman who opened the door was fat and sloppy with streaks of grey blonde hair sticking to her forehead. She wore a faded cotton dress, black, lace-up shoes and cotton stockings. "Yeah?" she said. "What do you want?"

"Mrs. Cross?"

"Hey, don't I know you?"

"You used to know me. My name's Jack Twining."

"Jack! Is it really you?" Her tone sounded phony. She pretended to care, but he saw no compassion or tenderness in her face. He'd run away once, depriving her of a couple of months of county aid. He was sure she still resented it.

"It's me."

"What brings you to this neck of the woods?"

"Looking for my mamma. You told me once you know who she is."

"That I did, honey, that I did."

"So can you tell me who she is, where she is?"

"I don't remember, but I can find out. All I gotta do is go down to the county offices."

"Can you call?" he asked, pleading with her and angry at himself for doing it.

"I can't do that, Jack honey," she said. "It's confidential information, and they won't give it out over the phone."

He was getting impatient now, angry. "Can't you try?"

"I'll tell you what. I'll go down there as soon as I can. This afternoon or tomorrow morning, okay?"

"I guess so."

"It's all I can do, Jack. You come back tomorrow, all right? I promise once I find out the name and address, I'll tell you. I'll even help you locate your mom...and your daddy too, if you like."

He didn't trust this bitch. There was something about the way she looked when she told him these things.

The next day he called.

"Where are you?" Mrs. Cross asked. "I've got what you want—names and addresses of your mama and your daddy. All you gotta do is stop over, and I'll give them to you."

"Can't you give 'em to me over the phone?"

"How can I help you look for them if I can't see you face-to-face?"

"You don't need to help me look. Hell, Mrs. Cross, if you have the addresses."

"Is that any way to talk, Jack? I'm just trying to help is all."

"Then do it. Tell me who they are and where they live."

"Where are you, Jackie?"

Had he heard someone whisper that very same question before she voiced it to him?

"Read me the names and addresses," he said.

"Jack, I gotta talk to you. So come on by. Are you far away?"

"Goddammit, give me the names!"

"I told you, hon, let's get together so's I can help. Make it easier for you."

"You bitch!" he screamed. "If you don't start giving me the names, I'm coming over all right. To fix your fucking ass."

"What now?" Jack heard her whisper.

The fucking cunt had gone to the cops! And they were right there waiting. Barely able to contain his rage, he slammed down the receiver. Had she lied all along? Maybe she had never known anything about his parents. Instead, like he'd always thought, she'd been sore at losing her income for that couple of months. To get even, she was trying to stick it to him! Fuck it to hell, he'd go over and blow her away!

He had all the guns from Smallen's payoff. He'd have no trouble offing her quick.

Still, there was the matter of the cops. If they were around, they'd be watching the house. Maybe they could trace him to the room. Maybe they knew who and where his con friend was. Shit!

The best thing to do was to hit the road. He'd miss Dee, but what the hell. That seemed to be turning sour too. She was a good woman. Maybe she could even have helped settle him down. But after the first few times they went out drinking, she'd stopped returning his calls. Hell, maybe he was getting paranoid. Probably she was just too damned busy.

He was almost out of cash, so he sold the Corvair to George Payne. Even that made him nervous. Maybe this guy had gone south on him too. He stole another Chevy, this time a black sedan, and headed out of town, alone as always.

He had no plans, didn't know where he was headed. The typical con, he thought. Always headed away from something. As he drove along through fields of wheat and corn, he had an idea. Maybe he'd look up his old buddy, Bobby Augustus Davis. If there was any other man he could trust on the face of the earth, it was Bobby Davis.

Jack remembered when they met at Leavenworth, him and Bobby. "Don't you know them initials spell B-A-D?" Jack had asked him. "Is that what you are?"

"You better believe it!" Bobby said.

Although Jack was easily an inch taller at five foot, eleven, and at 170, twenty or so pounds heavier than Bobby, he believed it. The cold blue eyes of the young con were uncompromising and tough. Yet Bobby had been young and innocent in the ways of penitentiary life. Soon, Jack knew, he was going to be forced into being a chicken for the chicken hawks unless he had him a sponsor. Jack decided to take care of him because nobody fucked with Twining. That being so, then nobody would fuck with Bobby either. That's the way it had been, and the two of them had gotten along fine.

Like most cons who stuck together, they made an agreement to look up one another once they both got out. Then, of course, Bobby had been transferred to Marion.

Jack would sure like to see him though. On the other hand, Jack was hotter than hell. If Bobby by chance had gone square, being with Jack could fuck him up good. Still and all, he *was* the only living soul that Jack felt anyways close to.

He headed west on Route 66. Driving within the limit, sleeping briefly along the side of rural roads, he made it to Oklahoma in two days. He called Bobby's dad in Ponca City. Floyd told him Bobby had gone to Houston. He gave him the address and phone number.

TWENTY-FOUR

George Michael Alleyn liked nothing better than sitting with his wife and two-and-a-half-year-old daughter Julie every morning and talking about his previous evening's activities. His war stories, as Shirley called it. She'd be ironing or folding clothes, Julie playing with her Barbie doll. More than likely Mike would be shining his leather gear or polishing his shoes.

He loved the CHP, truly loved it, not as much as he loved Shirley and Julie, of course, but pretty near.

"So," he was telling her one day, "I gave this guy a ticket. Danged shovel fell off his pickup and landed right in front of me on the road."

"You gave the poor guy a ticket," Shirley said. "You ought to be ashamed. I'm sure it wasn't deliberate, his losing the shovel."

"Gosh darn, Shirley. It bounced right over the patrol car. Could have hit the windshield. Could have caused a really bad accident. Lucky I was in a black-and-white. If I'd been on a motorcycle, it could have killed me. Don't you know that?"

"I hope you didn't get this excited at the man," Shirley said. "I pity the poor guy if you did."

"If I did! The darn fool deserved it! Whoever heard of a guy—" He looked up and saw she was grinning. She was kidding him again, and he'd let it get to him. That was Shirley all right. Great sense of humor. Maybe not as extroverted as he was, but certainly up on him in their verbal sparring.

Other than that, they were pretty much a matched pair, Mike thought. She was petite, and Mike was not a big man, not by a long shot. He'd barely passed the height requirement for joining the CHP. He remembered how concerned he'd been about that. "Think big," she told him. "Just think big, and you'll be big."

"Uh huh. I certainly believe that, Shirley. I can hardly wait for you to tell me another."

"You'll see," she said. "You'll pass with no problem."

As a guy whose height had been listed on various documents as anywhere from five, eight and a half to five, nine exactly, he took her advice. And as she'd said, there'd been no problem.

At twenty-three, Mike felt he had it made. Married to the best woman in the world, with one little girl and another baby on the way and with his career taking shape, life couldn't be better.

Mike came from Brownsville, Texas. When he was in eighth grade, his family moved to the Bay Area, his father transferred there by his employer United Airlines. So Mike had finished school in Campbell, a little community on the Peninsula just south of San Jose.

After high school, for lack of anything better, he enrolled in junior college and got a job as a technician for IBM. Then he met Shirley, and within a few months they were married. He figured his life was pretty well set. He'd finish his two years of school, get a promotion at his job, and that would be it. It was okay, comfortable. Like most young married couples, they were always a little short of cash, but someday they'd get ahead. All they had to do was wait.

Then everything changed. He'd come home from his last night class, turned on the local news and heard an announcement that said the CHP was hiring.

"Hey, hon, come here," he called to Shirley. She was in the kitchen finishing up the day's dishes.

"What is it?" she asked.

"Come here and listen?" He pointed to the TV screen and waited till the announcement was finished. "What do you think?" he asked. He didn't wait for a reply. "The CHP thing. Seems like something I could do."

"You and Broderick Crawford," she said not taking him seriously.

"Who?"

"You know, the guy who starred on that old TV series."

"What old series?"

"'Highway Patrol'."

"Never saw it," he said.

"You and he'd make a good team," she said, "riding off into the sunset each day in your cop car."

Mike had laughed then and let it go. He wanted to think about it a little more before the talk got serious.

The next day he still felt the same. Why not? He stopped after work and picked up the State application forms.

"I decided, Shirley, I'm going to apply." He handed her the forms.

"Apply?" she asked. "Apply for what?"

"The CHP. The Academy."

"I thought you were kidding."

"Maybe I was only half-serious; I don't know. But I've been thinking about it. So what do you say?"

"If that's what you really want, I guess you should do it."

"What I meant was will you type up the forms? You know I can't type worth a darn."

She rolled her eyes, then laughed and held out her hand. "Maybe they'll do another series," she said. "You and I'll be the stars. I can see it now." She held her hands in front of her like she was framing a landscape. "Shirley Alleyn and Mike Alleyn in 'I Married the CHP.' I'd be the star, of course. You'd have just a supporting role."

He turned the forms in. A few days later he was notified of an upcoming written test.

TWENTY-FIVE

To prepare for the oral board he'd need to pass to get into the Academy, Mike asked Shirley to drill him on a list of questions they felt were likely to be asked. On the day of the panels, Shirley took off work so she could go with him to San Francisco.

Knowing he'd be nervous, Mike smeared the palms of his hands with antiperspirant. While he went in, Shirley waited in Doggie Diner across the street.

The first part was easy—questions about his employment, his schooling, his home life. The three members of the panel asked him about his aspirations, his outlook, what dismayed him most about society. He decided the best way to get through this was to play a role—that of an enlightened conservative, a term he knew from a course in poli sci at San Francisco State.

"How about marijuana?" one of the panelists asked. "Do you think it should be legalized?"

"Well, sir," Mike said, "I don't think so. I think legalizing it would just give people another way of escaping responsibility. It couldn't help but compound problems that already exist. Alcoholism and things like that."

"What about taking another man's life in the course of duty?"

The question from the CHP captain startled Mike. He'd never considered such a thing in relation to himself. Yet newspapers were full of stories about police and suspects shooting it out.

"I... I don't know, sir " he said. "But I guess...it would depend on the circumstances."

"I suppose you know," the captain snapped, "that in a situation where deadly force must be used, you don't have time to think things through."

"I understand," Mike said. "I just... Well, I don't think I can give you a definite answer. Maybe once I think about it...." His voice trailed off.

"I certainly suggest you *do* that! We're not running a pansy outfit, you know. Since our founding in 1929, well over a hundred officers have lost their lives in the line of duty. Many from gunfire." He leaned forward. "And did you know—even though we're primarily a traffic control agency—that each year we arrest more than 10,000 felons! Many of them, as you well may imagine, do not want to be taken. If even one of our—"

"Thank you, Capt. Johnson!" the panel moderator said. "I'm sure Mr. Alleyn will be made thoroughly aware of the dangers and responsibilities of the job if and when he enters the Academy." The man turned to Mike. "Would you like to say anything further?"

Mike shook his head.

"That will be it then, Mr. Alleyn."

• • •

"Don't worry about it," Shirley said on the drive home. "Even if the captain didn't like what you said, the two civilians were probably more impressed than if you'd come across as some type of gunslinger."

"Maybe."

"You know," Shirley said, "I wasn't sure about this. How I felt or you felt."

"About joining the CHP?"

"I thought maybe it was some sort of romantic idea. The suggestive power of television. But I'm proud of you. I think you've made a good choice."

A few weeks later Mike was asked to come in for his physical. Only then did he learn he was nearsighted.

"Talk to an ophthalmologist," Shirley said. "See if he can suggest some exercises or something."

He passed the next eye exam and was fitted with contact lenses.

Twenty-Six

"I guess you're my break-in officer," Skip said as he held out his hand.

"Jack Conway. And you must be James Edward Pence, Jr.?"

At five feet nine, Skip was at minimum height for the CHP. He knew his stocky body made him appear shorter and perhaps even younger. A friend had once told him that short hair always made a guy look older. So he wore his short. His wife Jan disagreed. She told him it had just the opposite effect. He didn't know whether to believe her or not.

"Going to be warm today," Conway said. "Want to leave your coat in the office?"

"Sure." Skip's uniform was brand new, the first time he'd worn it. He took off the coat and stowed it in his locker.

It was May 29, 1969, and this was Skip's first day on the job. As he stepped outside, he saw that the sun was showing over the skyline of Newhall, a skyline formed by rolling hills and a smattering of houses.

"What do I call you, Jim or Junior?" Conway asked as they climbed into the black-and-white.

"I go by Skip. My grandpa started it. Called me his little skipper—" He broke off in embarrassment and glanced at Conway.

"Skip it is then," Conway said as he pulled off the grounds and out onto the roadway.

"We're working beat 14," Conway told him.

"Yes?" Skip was puzzled.

"Newhall is our dispatch point, right?"

"Right."

"All units assigned to this area have a primary number of 78. The second number is the beat you're working. Tomorrow, we may be working somewhere else. Then we'll be 78 followed by a different number. You'll catch on."

Maybe, Skip thought, by the time I've worked here twenty years.

"Look at that," Conway said and motioned toward an old dump truck going in the opposite direction. He pulled to the right shoulder, braked, and spun a U-turn, accelerating so quickly that the rear tires squealed on the pavement. "He's having trouble steering because of that heavy load."

"So are you going to take him?" Skip asked.

"Nope," Conway answered. "The way he's going, he'll most likely turn west on 126. He'll be within five miles of the scales, and we can legally order him in."

Skip mentally kicked himself for his stupidity. It was useless to stop an overweight truck if you weren't close to a scale. Well, that's why he had a break-in period and probation, he thought. Gave guys time to learn the things the Academy didn't teach.

Just as the truck reached Highway 99, Conway signaled the driver to stop. Before Skip had unfastened his seat belt, Conway was out of the car and on his way.

"Yes, sir, I agree," the driver was saying when Skip finally made it up to the truck, "I probably have too much gravel. But where I loaded up there wasn't no scale."

The driver said he'd loaded the gravel himself out in the desert, that he was building a house for his family. Wanted his kids away from street gangs and other bad influences.

The truck's windshield was cracked, the taillights burned out, and the whole thing looked like it would fall apart right there on the side of the road. Skip was amazed when Conway let the man go.

"Man!" Skip said as the truck pulled away. "That thing was full of violations. Aren't we supposed to cite him?"

The sun was becoming brighter. Conway took his sunglasses from his pocket and cleaned them with his necktie. "What you say is true," he said. "But the way I figure it, a guy has to feel good about what he's doing. Pinching that poor guy wouldn't have made me feel good. Sure, we could have loaded him up with violations, but what good would it have done? It wouldn't have made the truck any safer 'cause I'm sure he wouldn't have fixed it. He wouldn't have had the money. Anyhow here's a little bit of Conway philosophy. You ready."

Skip smiled. "Ready." By this time they were back on the road.

"When I pull out at the start of shift, I figure there are plenty of assholes deserving of tickets. They're the ones I'm after—the mothers who don't give a shit about the rest of us, who think they own the world, who rob and steal, who kill and injure others." He glanced quickly at Skip. "And you know, I think that guy really was trying to better his lot."

"'Wanting to work is so rare a want it should be encouraged.'"

"Is that a quote or something?"

"Abraham Lincoln. He's kind of a hobby of mine. Your philosophy's kind of like his."

By now they'd pulled onto the Antelope Valley Freeway and headed east toward Palmdale. "We'll run the beat one time and come back to Solemint Junction for coffee. What do you say?" Conway asked.

Skip squinted into the morning sun. Gotta get me some shades, he thought. Whoever heard of a Highway Patrolman without any shades?

"Shee-it!" Conway exclaimed. "Look at that Mustang! Doin' at least a hundred!"

The car was headed west on the other side of the divider. It seemed like it was tiptoeing, an effect caused by the lift of air as it neared take-off speed.

For the second time Skip was amazed. Conway did nothing; didn't slacken speed or attempt to give chase. He just kept driving east.

"Aren't we going to get him?"

"First, we have to get a clock. To do that, we have to be sneaky." He kept glancing into the rearview mirror. "He's out of sight, so hang on!" He braked hard and pulled to the left, into the gravel divider. The car did a near-perfect broadside, ending up accelerating westbound on the other side of the freeway.

"You have to let them get out of sight before you turn on them. Otherwise, they're going to slow down." Conway's voice was nearly drowned out by the roar of the Dodge's 440 engine.

The speedometer rose steadily to 110 and then climbed higher. The windshield wipers vibrated.

"There he is!" shouted Conway.

Ahead Skip saw the rear of the cream-colored Mustang. As they closed in, Conway slowed the patrol car. "Let's try him at 95! Keep a good eye on him. See if we gain, or he pulls away."

"Looks like he's pulling away."

"Yeah, but not bad. Let's do him for 95. You write them for a hundred plus, and the judge wants them to bring a toothbrush."

Once more the car lurched forward. This time the red light was on. As they pulled to within fifty yards of the Mustang, the brake lights flashed, and the driver signaled a stop.

"You take him," Conway said. "I'll bet he's been to 'Lost Wages' and has to be in L. A. to get to work at eight."

Skip got out and approached the left side of the car, scanning the rear seat as he went, stopping just before the trailing edge of the driver's door—gun hand free.

His knees shook. He wasn't sure if it was because of the upcoming encounter or the wild ride he'd experienced.

"Can I see your driver's license, please?" The driver didn't respond. "Sir, can I see your driver's license, please?"

"Ask him to roll down the window," Conway called from the other side of the car.

Skip tapped the window with his knuckles, and the man rolled it down.

"What's the trouble, officer?"

"We stopped you for speeding. Do you have a license?"

"A license to speed?" The man chuckled. When Skip didn't answer, he pulled out a driver's license.

Skip took it and the vehicle registration and returned to the right front of the patrol car where Conway assisted him in filling out the citation. The driver got out and approached them. "How fast was I going?" he asked.

"We clocked you at better than ninety-five," Conway told him.

"Bull shit! I couldn't have been going that fast. I may have drifted up to seventy-five coming down the hill, but no faster!"

"You were going quite a bit faster the mile or so we were behind you," retorted Conway.

"I thought that you didn't have a speed limit out here," the man said.

"How's that?" Conway asked.

"I thought Nevada didn't have a maximum speed limit. That's why I was cruising along. Nothing unsafe out here in the desert."

"I see. You've been driving along, wide awake and alert, perfectly aware of your surroundings."

"I'd never deliberately break the law."

"If you're so alert, you ought to know you left Nevada more than a hundred miles back. In California, the normal speed limit's sixty-five. Right here the limit's seventy."

"I guess it wouldn't do much good to fight this then, huh?"

Conway shook his head as they got back into the Dodge. "Nevada? Jesus! Just like on TV, eh?"

Skip didn't pay much attention. He had written his first speeding ticket and was a member of the brotherhood with his very own war story.

TWENTY-SEVEN

At twenty-three, married, with a two-year-old and another child on the way, Skip Pence saw no future in continuing as a welder at the Mare Island Naval Shipyards. Ever since making journeyman, he'd hated the repetitiveness of the tasks and couldn't see spending years at the job as his father had. He thought that applying to attend the CHP academy would improve his lot in life.

In some respects the decision had been an easy one. Skip's dad had been a truck driver. When he was injured in an accident, he moved the family from Chicago to California to take the same sort of job his son now had. Skip knew his dad wanted more for him than being stuck in a nine-to-five box. He told Skip he missed the highway.

"With you on the Highway Patrol," he said, "a part of me still can travel that road."

Skip knew his mother was proud of his decision, as was his younger brother. Jan was too, but when he told her he was going to fill out the forms, she was surprised.

It was a warm day. They were out back where Teresa was splashing in the wading pool.

"Why are you surprised?" he asked.

"You've always been a quiet kind of person, Skip. Introspective."

"Is that bad?"

She laughed. "I suppose not. But it seems that all the cops I've met are just the opposite. I always imagine that they like to race motorcycles and to sky dive. That they belong to bowling leagues and softball teams and can name every pro quarterback on every team for the past twenty years."

"So do you want that kind of a husband?" he teased.

"I'll tell you what kind of husband I want." He looked at her inquiringly. "I want the kind who played tuba in the high school band, whose hobbies are writing poetry and quoting Abe Lincoln. Think I can find that kind of person?"

"Wouldn't be surprised," he said.

"A guy who'd rather play with his daughter or play old Beach Boy songs on the guitar."

They'd both attended Armijo High in Fairfield, but in her senior year her family moved to Minnesota. She and Skip kept in touch, and when she graduated, he took off for Duluth where he and Jan were married.

Although the decision to join the CHP was easy, it was hard as well. At times Skip doubted he should follow through. He was a man with strong family feelings. And it was particularly rough when a new baby boy—James Dean Pence, named for his grandfather—was born just twenty days before Skip was supposed to leave.

He knew that once he graduated, more than likely they'd have to leave the area. He'd lived there since his family had moved from Chicago. It was beautiful, he thought, bordered by the Carquinez Straights on the south and the Napa wine country on the west. He felt reluctant to leave. So did Jan who'd been born there. It seemed a big step to trade their home and the closeness of family and friends.

Then all he had to do was look at Jan, whom he compared to a young Doris Day, and he knew she deserved better than what she had. His kids deserved better. And the doubts disappeared.

In January of 1969 he reported to the Academy. And he had to admit that even then there were times he wasn't sure if he'd made the right decision.

"Overall," he told Jan, "I like it. I really do. I don't mean to sound like I'm just spouting off. But what they say is true. It builds your confidence. It's like what you're doing really matters."

He knew beyond a doubt he was becoming a better man for his Academy experience. Yet, one part of being a peace officer bothered him. Carrying a gun and knowing he might have to take someone's life. A religious man, he discussed it with his pastor. "If your faith is strong," the minister told him, "God surely will direct you when the time comes."

• • •

He finished the training, went through the graduation ceremony, and here he and Jan and the kids were. Their mobile home had been moved to Saugus a week before, and Jan already had applied for a job at Doctor's Hospital in Panorama City.

TWENTY-EIGHT

Between 1966 and 1970 the CHP doubled its size. There were at least a couple of reasons. The Patrol had taken over responsibility for traffic control on the entire California freeway system, even inside incorporated cities. There was a new program of on-highway vehicle inspection performed by teams of CHP officers throughout the state. And, although it was never stated explicitly, many believed the real reason was so there could be a reserve of trained officers who could be called upon to assist in large-scale civil disobedience.

Rumors were rampant that doubling the Patrol's size was a bad move, that training at the Academy had deteriorated due to doubled-up classes and crowding, that young, inexperienced officers were breaking in the new cadets, that fledglings were working as partners. It would be only a matter of time, it was said, until they got in over their heads.

Neither Roger nor Walt agreed with this assessment. They'd had good training, and, even though their break-in officers had less than a year's experience, they'd fared well. Consistently working nights, they'd made their share of felony arrests and "hot stops." They'd picked up twenty to thirty drunk drivers each month and had never had a close call.

They'd discussed the possibility of being taken hostage but had pretty much set the thought aside as being too remote.

One night, a few weeks after they'd become partners and were working the night shift, Roger glanced over at Walt who was driving. "Remember," he said, "that at the Academy they told us we should work out some sort of plan if a guy we've stopped pulls a gun on one of us."

"Just tell me, Rog. Would you give up your gun in that kind of situation?"

"Maybe. Who knows?" He grinned. "Tell you what. If it's me up there, you go ahead and give up your gun. If it's you they got the drop on and I'm back here at the car, we'll try our plan."

Roger couldn't see any obscene gesture in the darkness of the car, but he was pretty sure there was one.

TWENTY-NINE

Every year across the United States an increasing number of policemen were killed, many of them shot. There'd even been a recent shoot-out in the Newhall area. A driver stopped for speeding shot Officer Warren Loftus in the stomach. The driver thought he was being stopped in connection with a robbery in Los Angeles rather than for a traffic violation. Loftus recovered, and the man was sent to prison for attempted murder.

Still it was strange, Walt mused, but no officer he knew thought much about death. At least not his own. You were surrounded by violence and death as part of the job, but somehow it didn't relate to what might happen to you.

Shortly after Loftus was shot, Walt and Nicki went back to Merced for a visit. Walt's father insisted he quit the Patrol, return home, and go into full partnership in the service stations.

"I know you like your job," his father said as Gabby bounced into the living room to crawl onto Walt's lap. "But I need you to help me out. Tom's got a good job teaching down at Soledad Prison. Bob has a future as a forest ranger, and I want Billy to stay in school."

"I know that, Dad. But you don't understand...."

He held up a hand. "Let me finish. The U-haul and Avis rentals are really booming. Besides..."

"What?"

"Your mom and I worry. The roads are filled with crazy people. Didn't Nicki even say that one of your friends got shot?"

Gabby pulled at Walt's ear. "Dad, it's something I can't say yes to."

"Think about it. Will you promise me that?"

"I promise. But the truth of the matter is I've been thinking of trying to switch to downtown L. A."

• • •

On the way home that evening, Walt brought up the subject with Nicki.

"Its really up to you," she said. "It's your job, your future. Sure, it would be nice for the girls to live near our folks, but that's not the only consideration."

THIRTY

Jack decided they needed a car and talked Bobby into going to a lot and picking one out. They found a red '64 Pontiac with white leather upholstery and less than 60,000 miles. Bobby pulled Jack aside and said they should talk.

"What is it?" Jack asked.

"It's going to look suspicious if we plunk down all that cash."

The sun and the slight breeze had cleaned the smog from the air.

"So what are we going to do? I sure like that car."

He hesitated. "Do you think maybe it's a little too flashy? The sort people are going to remember."

"Jesus Christ, let's just buy the fucking car!"

"I think we should get us some traveler's checks first. Use them instead of cash."

"You got ID?"

"My own."

"Jesus, Bobby, you want the feds and whoever else to be able to trace us?"

"So what are we going to do?"

"Before I left Winston-Salem I picked up this dumb fuck's ID."

"Whose ID we talking about?"

"I was reading the want ads and saw this ad for some tools."

"What in the hell you want with tools?"

"I never said anything about wanting tools."

"What is this about then?"

"You're pissing me off Bobby, you know that?"

"I'm sorry."

"Anyhow, I called the man and asked to come over and see his tools. Before you say anything, I was just checking things out."

"The house?"

"Yeah, like it's only dumb johns who advertise things in the paper. I always figured it's an open invitation. So I looked at his tools—nice collection, all right. He was getting rid of them 'cause he didn't have no energy anymore. Said he'd get home from work and didn't feel like doing nothing but propping up his feet on the coffee table and watching a little TV. I sympathized and all that. Then I told him I needed time to consider whether I could afford to spend as much money as he was asking. What do you think I saw there besides them tools?"

"How the hell would I know?"

"Guns, man. A .44 magnum carbine, two .45 automatic pistols, and I don't know what all. Figured they might come in handy."

"They the ones you used when we robbed that market in Houston?"

"You got it." He and Bobby had hit a Krogers and picked up $7,200 and made a getaway by stealing a car off a nearby lot.

"Anyhow," Jack went on, "I waited till Sunday and went back to the house. Just like I hoped, no one was there. Off to church, Sunday dinner at the kids' house, who knows what? That's how I got them."

"But what about the ID?"

"The dumb fuck had left his wallet on the dresser. I took his driver's license is all. Maybe he hasn't even missed it."

"And that's what you're going to let me use."

"You'll going to be Mr. Talbert. Russell Lowell Talbert, III."

They hailed a taxi and Bobby asked for the nearest banking establishment. The driver told them there was a nearby branch of Security First National. Once there, they asked the taxi to wait, and Bobby traded his money for checks. They headed back to the lot and signed over the traveler's checks to buy the car.

Bobby said they might as well go to the DMV and get a license. Jack told Bobby to go ahead. He wasn't sure he could pass the driver's test himself. Hadn't ever had much chance to drive. Besides, he didn't want ID in his own name. He was a federal parole violator, and he figured things like driver's license applications were checked.

Using Talbert's license, Bobby passed the test, and the two of them took off, heading north along the coast on Highway 101. Plenty of cash and nothing to do but enjoy it.

Jack looked at the hitchhikers who lined the freeway ramps and wondered aloud where they all were going.

"Don't know," Bobby answered. "Don't much care. But if we see a couple of sharp-looking chicks, let's be sure and give them a lift."

Well, Jack hoped they wouldn't see those chicks. No sense getting involved. Now that he and Bobby were on their way, he didn't want to get messed up with no runaway kids. There sure were a lot of them though, and they all looked dirty as hell.

THIRTY-ONE

Jack Twining had always been tough and strong as an ox. He knew his sinewy build and menacing disposition had kept most people at a distance. Walt Mollett had been different. When they'd first crossed paths at Atlanta, Jack had been only twenty, pulling thirty years for the bank robbery. Mollett, twenty-nine or thirty, had been looking for a cute guy. Jack wanted no part of being a queen. If he was going to be a homo, he'd be a daddy. His time in previous joints and his record of noncooperation with the Man gave him this status.

Mollett never took him on at Atlanta. But one day in the yard at Alcatraz they came to blows. One morning a couple of weeks later Jack was working in the dry cleaning shop. Mollett slipped away from his job in the laundry and into the room where Jack was working alone. Mollett had a knife.

"Okay, you son-of-a-bitch, I've been after you for years, and I've come to claim what's mine. You don't do as I say, I'm going to cut off your balls and stuff them in your mouth."

"You friggin' asshole," Jack screamed jumping the man, hardly even aware of the knife he held in his hand. Jack grabbed Mollett around the neck and started to choke, but Mollett shoved him away to get room to try to use his knife. A butter knife he'd stolen a couple of weeks ago and honed to lethal sharpness.

Jack jumped out of the way and hit him on the back of the neck with clasped hands. Somewhere along the way the knife got lost, and it was just the brute strength of two men of nearly equal size and ability.

Jack lashed out and knocked Mollett down. His head hit the stand of the mangle press, stunning him. Jack grabbed him around the neck and pounded his head hard into the unyielding piece of equipment. He stopped only when he was sure Mollett wasn't going to get up anymore.

Suddenly, guards were all over Jack. But it didn't matter. All he cared about was that Mollett lay still—his skull crushed.

Jack had spent the next thirty days in D block. The longest month of his life. Total isolation. No light and no cell furniture. One meal a day. A shower with a half hour exercise each week.

Jack had been brought out twice, once to tell his story to an assistant warden and then again to FBI agents. Finally, he was taken to the mainland for a hearing. It was ruled that the homicide had been justifiable. The verdict was that he'd killed Mollett in self-defense. A few days later, Jack was returned to second-grade status—a regular cell, three meals, no work, just confinement. A month later he made first-grade and went back to his old job. For the next six months, he kept knives handy, hidden on whichever side of the detector he was on. One in the shop, one in the cell and one in the yard. Even had a guy keeping one for him in the mess hall.

Carswell Wins on Nomination Test

Story in Cols. 1-2

HERALD EXAMINER

8 STAR
LATEST SPORTS

TODAY'S
COMPLETE NEW YORK
AND AMERICAN STOCKS

4 CHP OFFICERS SLAIN

One Suspect Kills Self; Nab Second

The Los Angeles Herald-Examiner *and other newspapers, both in and out of California, carried the tragic story on their front pages Monday, April 6, 1970.*

Roger D. Gore

Walter C. Frago

James E. Pence, Jr.

George M. Alleyn

CHP officers Roger Gore and Walt Frago, responding to a report of a motorist brandishing a firearm, stopped a red Pontiac at J's Coffee Shop near present-day Magic Mountain Parkway.

James Pence and George "Mike" Alleyn radioed Gore and Frago that they would roll in behind them as backup.

By age 34, Jack Wright Twining had been in eight federal prisons, including the notorious Alcatraz where he killed another inmate in a fight eventually ruled self-defense.

Twining didn't have much of a plan in traveling back to California. He and Davis bounced from San Francisco to Sacramento to Southern California looking for an easy mark, perhaps in a bank or a market, but finally settled on an armored car.

Bobby Augustus Davis had been paroled to Houston, Texas less than nine months before he and Twining arrived in California. Davis obtained a California driver's license under the name Russell Lowell Talbert III by using a license Twining had stolen in Winston-Salem, North Carolina.

Concerned the used-car salesman would become suspicious if they used cash, Twining and Davis paid for this 1964 red Pontiac with traveler's checks.

J's Coffee Shop and the adjacent Standard gas station were popular stopping-off places near Interstate Highway 5 at Henry Mayo Drive.

In the well-lighted access area, the vehicles, suspects and officers were clearly visible to witnesses including twenty-four young members of the Del Aire Assembly of God Church Choir.

In this photo the two police cruisers and the red Pontiac can be seen in the lower left corner, J's Coffee Shop in the center and Interstate 5 along the top.

J's Coffee Shop and the Standard gas station catered to travelers passing along Interstate 5. In the middle photo, Pence and Alleyn's unit 78-12 is in the foreground with Gore and Frago's 78-8 behind it. The photo on the right shows unit 78-12.

Sometime during the melee, the Pontiac's rear window was shot out and its left rear tire flattened. The crime scene investigation continued well past dawn.

The photo at the right shows the arsenal Twining and Davis had amassed to use in their crimes.

After fleeing on foot, Twining took Steven Hoag hostage in Hoag's home. Hoag lived 3½ miles from J's Coffee Shop but, coincidentally, only a few hundred yards north of the Newhall area CHP patrol office. Steven's wife, Betty, managed to phone the CHP office. Within minutes the home was cordoned off by both CHP and L.A. County Sheriff officers.

When a Sheriff's assault team entered the house under cover of a tear gas barrage, Twining, shown here shortly after, put the muzzle of the shotgun he'd taken from Officer Frago beneath his chin and pulled the trigger. The deputies returned fire believing the suspect had shot at them.

Awakened as he slept in a camper mounted on his pickup, Daniel Schwartz exchanged shots with Bobby Davis when Davis ordered him out of the camper.

Davis, now out of ammunition, threatened to set the camper on fire then severely beat Schwartz when he emerged. A short time later, at a roadblock set up by Sheriff officers, Davis—who had been wounded by one of Schwartz' shots—surrendered without incident.

The tragic deaths of the four officers wasn't completely in vain. Because of the Newhall incident, major procedural changes—including the way an officer approaches a car, the use of bulletproof vests and the methods used to place suspects under arrest—have been implemented by police agencies across the United States. Experts say these changes have helped thousands of other officers, saving lives and avoiding serious injuries.

PART TWO
CONVERGENCE

Thirty-Two

"This is great!" Jack said flashing a rare smile. "There's something about the ocean, and the hills and the sky that makes life worth living. Worth hanging on to!"

"Can't beat Southern California for location and weather," Bobby replied.

"Can't beat being on the outside," Jack said. "Let's see," he mumbled counting on his fingers. "Sixteen months, isn't that pathetic?"

"What is?" Bobby asked, not much interested, concentrating instead on his driving. They'd been on the road all day. As they neared the outskirts of San Jose, traffic was picking up.

"Only sixteen months." He shook his head as if in disbelief. "I've spent only sixteen months on the outside since I was a kid.

"Is that so?" Bobby decided to humor Jack. He knew from experience if he didn't, the result would be sullenness and barely repressed anger.

"Did my first hard time when I was sixteen. Burglary. In Butler, P.A. I was stupid then. They got me trying to sell a couple of portable radios out on the street. That wasn't my first time in trouble. When I was twelve, thirteen, I started knocking over truckers sleeping alongside the highway. Pulling a gun on them, taking their money. Then I rode off on my bike. Got caught then too, but I was so young they let me go."

Bobby nodded absently. He'd heard it all before. Many times, if the truth be told. Sitting in the recreation hall or having a smoke in the yard. But you didn't interrupt a story or mention you'd heard it before. Even when you knew it to be way too preposterous, you didn't say anything. That was because in prison, one of the few things a man has is his memories. His image of himself and of better times past. To destroy or challenge that memory made you as bad as the Man.

"How come you started getting in trouble so young?" Bobby asked. He knew the answer, but it was good to keep Jack talking. Bobby sensed that talking about his past somehow relieved the pressure that was continually housed inside him, the catlike nervousness that could explode in violent outbursts. And Bobby had seen what that temper could do. Totally uncontrolled and uncontrollable. Damaging to whatever it was directed toward.

"Hell, I don't know, Bobby. A victim of my environment, I guess." Jack chuckled. "I must have been about six or so when they took me out of the orphanage and put me in a foster home. I ended up with this lady who hated kids. I swear she did. There were usually two or three of us boys. She put up with us just 'cause the county paid her to do it. The other kids kept coming and going. Adopted or sent to other homes. I never was. I stayed there till I was fourteen. Then I went to the reformatory for running away. God, they treated you rough. You know how jails in the south were then. The last time they sent me back to the foster home, I did it right. I stole a car and got clear off to Chicago. Because I was still on juvenile probation, they had a fugitive warrant as well as the interstate transportation of a stolen car beef waiting for me. Christ, they were looking for me in West Virginia, Tennessee—that's where I got the car—and in Winston-Salem. I was only seventeen. Picked me up on my birthday there in Chicago. Got stopped for making a turn where you wasn't supposed to. Sent me to the federal reformatory in El Reno, Oklahoma, on a three-year, six-month Dyer Act." He grinned. "You might say that was the turning point in starting my life downhill.

"Well, enough of this crap," Jack said. "What kind of score are we going to try to make out here? Another market, you think?" He fingered the .45 automatic pistol shoved in his waistband and concealed by his untucked shirt.

"Whatever looks good, old buddy. Maybe a bank, or an armored car. I've always thought an armored car would be easy. They carry lots of cash and the guards are usually second-rate dildos. All you got to do is ambush one of them and then turn it over." He glanced over at Jack. "We'll be in Frisco tonight and take a look around."

Jack fidgeted, feeling the grip of the gun at his waist and winding his watch. A Bulova. He told Bobby it was one of the items he'd stolen from old Russell Lowell Talbert, III.

• • •

For Bobby, the skyline of San Francisco was something special. He'd been there twice before. Once while he'd waited for his buddy to be mustered out of the Marine Corps; another time on the run from the FBI for the bank job in Temple, Georgia. He'd stayed a couple of months then, really cooling it. He'd even enrolled in computer school. Then, as Christmas neared, he'd gotten homesick, missing his first wife Joan. A strange city, no matter how exciting, was no place to spend Christmas alone. He called and let Joan and his parents talk him into returning for the holidays and turning himself in right after. A few months inside they said, then parole. Things would work out.

Shit, he'd been given twelve years. Like Jack, his first federal rap had landed him in El Reno, and Joan had divorced him soon after. You did dumb things when you were young.

· · ·

Jack knew how Bobby felt about San Francisco. He'd told him often enough. Jack felt exactly the opposite. Any fascination for the City's landmarks was far overshadowed by the existence of a small twelve-acre island, named for pelicans, situated one and a quarter miles due west of the City. Alcatraz, the American Devil's Island.

Jack had spent just short of five years of his life in those brooding buildings, number 1362-A2. Now, at the mere thought of it, he felt his stomach constrict, causing pain so bad that his eyes watered.

"Let's keep going," he said.

"We just got here. I know this town pretty well. Come on, Jack, let me show you the sights—"

"Goddammit, let's go. I don't even give a shit where. Just get out of this fucking town!"

"Okay, okay, take it easy. I'll look for a way back to the freeway."

As once more they pulled onto Highway 101 and headed north across Golden Gate Bridge, Jack allowed himself a look to the left. It was dark now, and due to traffic in the opposing lane, he couldn't see much out in the direction of the ocean. What? he thought. Were those lights out there? Again, the sick feeling as the memories came rushing back.

The boat trip across the choppy waters. Being manacled. The dreary, overcast sky. Being greeted on the dock by armed guards. Being strip searched.

The main entrance to the bastion was through three high-security observation rooms. There were five guard towers on the catwalks of the high wall, each housing men cradling high-powered rifles. Strategic placement of the towers permitted observation of the entire complex and all its approaches. Welcome to the cage! A fortress built in 1853 to keep people out; its purpose altered in 1868 to becoming a military stockade to keep people in.

Routine. Up at 6:30, down to chow, back to cell for count, to the dry cleaning shop, lunch at 11:30 sharp, back for count, back to dry cleaning soldier-boy uniforms at 1:00, dinner at 5:00, final lockup and count at 5:30, lights out at 9:30, talk, smoke, think, sleep.

Saturday and Sunday walk in the recreation yard. Occasionally, a movie. Visitors permitted. No one had ever visited him.

None of the several prisons he had been in before or since held the dread of Alcatraz. He'd earned his assignment there as a result of a thwarted escape attempt while in Atlanta in March of 1958. He and another inmate, Billy Reed, had manufactured a counterfeit key which had let them into a locked security closet in the prison hospital. They'd already moved a metal locker and had started a tunnel down through the floor and out toward the wall. They'd gone nine feet deep and twenty-two feet long, still sixty feet away from the outside wall. Then they'd been discovered. Reed had been given solitary and Jack had been sent to Alcatraz.

The time he spent on the rock had been the hardest and most depressing of Jack's incarcerations. The strict security, the isolation, the icy, foreboding waters and continual fog created a sense of total helplessness. As the time passed, each day was exactly like the one before. And worse was the promise that tomorrow would be still the same. The dreariness saturated a man's bones and flowed into the soul itself.

Once the car started to climb the hills on the Marin side of the Bay, Jack began breathing more easily.

"Hey man," he told Bobby, "I'm sorry for gettin' all pushed out of shape back there. I don't know, I just can't explain it. So many times, I looked across at the lights of San Francisco and thought about all those square johns living it up, drinking, screwing. It kind of makes you crazy. Makes you really hate them."

Jack paused and looked back at the disappearing city lights. "I wonder if the Indians are still down there on the island," he said. "They took over the place. Moved in—a whole damn tribe—and the government couldn't stop them. Shut off their lights and water and still they stayed. Hope they keep it, that's all that place is good for. Give it back to the Indians."

"Let's stay over here on the coast for a couple days," Bobby said, "and then head into Sacramento. That's the state capitol and a pretty good-sized town, I hear."

"Maybe we'll find what we want there," Jack answered. He leaned his head against the back of the seat and closed his eyes.

Thirty-Three

It was a two-car collision. A bad one. A 1966 Chevrolet going southbound had veered to its left. It crossed the dirt divider strip where it was met at a right angle by a northbound Mercury station wagon. Hit broadside at a point just to the front of the passenger door, the Chevrolet had spun to its right and made a second impact with the left side of the Mercury. The driver of the Mercury wagon had been catapulted into the steering wheel and windshield of his vehicle and killed immediately, his scalp torn back to a point even with the ear. The second impact caused ejection of the middle-aged woman in the right front of the Chevrolet. She died when her head hit the highway at sixty miles per hour.

A third vehicle, following the Mercury, ran over the body as it rolled down the highway. This vehicle had failed to stop.

"Get out some flares! I'll check the victims!" Roger yelled. "But watch out for spilled gas!"

Walt raced to the trunk of the patrol car. He pulled out the first-aid kit and laid it on the left rear fender in the event Roger needed it. He grabbed the flares and lighted them.

"Oh, my God." Roger shined his flashlight into the Mercury and then onto the pulp in the roadway. No question they were dead.

His first view into the torn and twisted metal of the Chevrolet deepened his horror. The driver, a middle-aged man, obese and balding, was hopelessly crushed by the steel framework of the car. Even over the din of an approaching ambulance, Roger could hear the wail of a girl. She looked to be about fourteen and was trapped in the rear seat, right leg wedged under the front seat which had come off the track and was now near the rear deck of the vehicle. She was crying hysterically and flailing both arms inches from the back of the dead man, probably her father. One leg, the free one, had a compound fracture. Roger could see the femur poking through the girl's slacks just above the knee, The area was saturated with blood. The girl's arms hit again and again against sharp edges of metal and chrome. They already were severely lacerated.

Roger felt a wave of nausea. No matter how many you see, he thought, they still affected you. The appearance: blood, glass, flashing lights, twisted wrecks and ruined bodies. The smells: human excrement, blood, burning phosphorous from the flares, gas, grease, and death. The sounds: crying, screaming, sirens, yelling, dying. You never got used to it.

The girl's moaning brought him back as he fought his shock and revulsion. "It's going to be all right now," he told her. His training and experience began to take hold, and he felt control coming back.

"Got a live one over here!" he yelled to the ambulance crew which was just arriving.

He glanced in at the girl. She had reduced her cries to a low whine of pain. She stared back at him, doe-eyed, trapped—fear, pain and sorrow reflected by the beam of his flashlight. And, at the same time, trust and faith.

"Help me! Help me! Please!" she began again. Her arms began to swing about more violently against the debris.

"Hold on! Just hold on! We'll have you out in a minute," he told her trying to reach into the wreck to grab her arms.

The next forty minutes were the longest in Roger's life. Because of the crushed condition of the Chevrolet, neither the girl nor the body of her father could be extricated. By leveling himself into the gaping hole in the left side of the wreckage, Roger could hold both arms of the girl. He managed to wrap a bandage around the broken leg to immobilize it. As he lay there partly on his side and stomach, his face near the girl's, he once again fought nausea. The dead father's head was also now near his own. The back of the neck looked gray. It looked stiff and cold.

The only way to try to get the vehicles separated enough to rescue the girl and pull out the body was to use two tow trucks going in opposite directions.

"Roger, you better get clear!" It was Walt's voice.

Good old Walt. Steady, sure, Walt. There was some reason and sanity in the goddamned world. Here in all this chaos was Walt. Taking statements from witnesses. Making measurements and drawing a diagram. Taking pictures and gathering facts for a report, and completing an investigation. Giving directions to ambulance, tow and fire personnel. Calling the coroner and attending to the innumerable details involved in handling a thing like this.

"Sure partner, thanks," said Roger as he eased himself out of the totaled vehicle.

• • •

When Roger arrived home at 7:30, Valerie was stirring up Cream of Wheat for Janine. "You're late."

He saw a concerned look in her. "Crash up by Lake Hughes Road," he said.

"A bad one?" she asked.

Roger unbuckled the Sam Brown belt and swung his gun onto the couch. "Two dead, one injured. We spent the night working on it."

"Want to talk about it or go to bed?" she asked.

"Nothing to talk about," he told her. "One guy lost control—fell asleep or whatever—and crossed the divider. The other car took him broadside."

Roger took a hot shower and went to bed. It was a long time before sleep came.

Thirty-Four

"Birds must fly upside down here," Jack said. They'd reached Sacramento and were looking for a place to stay.

"Why's that?" Bobby said.

"Cause there sure ain't nothing worth shitting on here on the ground."

Bobby glanced at him in the gathering darkness. At least Jack's mood was improving. It was a little wearing to have him always ready to bite off your head.

They pulled up to an apartment house just off Stockton Boulevard. A sign out front advertised a heated pool and furnished apartments for fifty-one dollars a month.

"What do you think?" Bobby said.

"'Florin East Garden Apartments.' "Why don't we go find out?"

• • •

"Good morning, ma'am," Bobby said. "My name's Russ Talbert, and this is my partner James Nash."

"Pleased to meet you boys," the woman answered. "I'm Mrs. Laura Sammas. Been managing the place now ever since it opened."

"Is that right?" Bobby said. "Judging by how things look, it seems to me, Mrs. Sammas, you've done a mighty fine job."

"Why thank you, Mr. Talbert. It's a pleasure to meet such polite young men as you two are."

"Our pleasure, ma'am," Jack said.

"Is this long term or short term rental?" Mrs. Sammas asked.

Bobby and Jack exchanged glances. "Short term, I'd say," Jack answered. "We just want to get our bearings and look around before we move our families here."

"You boys both married then."

"Yes, ma'am," Bobby answered. "Carmel and me are expecting. That's why she didn't come along."

"Your first?"

"The first one."

"What about you, Mr. Nash?"

"Two kids, both in school. My wife and I, we talked it over and thought it best if I came out first. So since me and Russ have been pals for a time, we decided to share expenses."

Bobby could tell the woman was impressed. "You'll be wanting a furnished place then," she said.

"Right ma'am," Bobby answered.

"Got just the thing. Corner apartment, windows on two sides. Come on, I'll show you." She led them into a center court and up a set of steps. She said there'd be a thirty-five dollar cleaning deposit and three dollars for the key.

They said they'd take it, and she asked them to fill out a rental agreement. Bobby hoped she didn't notice that he transposed the license number of the car from OSY 805 to OYS 805. Even if she did ever notice, Bobby figured, she'd write it off as a simple mistake.

The following day, a Wednesday, Bobby and Jack went downtown to the State Library.

"I'm a salesman," Bobby told the young woman working the desk. "I'm trying to identify a few of the important people in Sacramento. So do you happen to have a book that lists them?"

"You mean professional people—politicians, judges, people like that?

"That's right."

"I think I know the very thing," she said, and guided him and Jack to a nearby shelf that held the California Blue Book.

Bobby thanked her, picked up the book and looked under the heading of "Bankers." There he found the names and business addresses of bank managers and executives throughout the city. Pulling a pen and a note pad from his pocket, he copied down a few names.

"What's all this for?" Jack asked.

"I learned this from a guy in Marion. We have their names and place of business, right?"

"What the hell good does that do?"

"Now we go back and look them up in the phone book so we'll have their home address, as well. If we decide to, we can take them en route or even hold the family at home while we contact the guy at the bank. With this information, there are lots of angles."

Back at the apartment, Jack offered to try to match the names to home addresses.

"I'm going to go get some smokes," Bobby said. "See you in a bit." He went outside and down to the pool area where he'd seen a cigarette vending machine. Even though it was late March, the weather was mild and the temperature in the mid-seventies. Bobby bought a pack of Camels and sat down to watch two young girls splash in the water.

He thought about what he and Jack were going to do to be able to make a big score. Kidnap a bank official or his family and demand a lot of money? Probably. As soon as it was done, he'd go back to Carmel and the baby. From then on he was going to go straight. Leastways after he had enough money to buy the nursing home he dreamed of running.

He and his buddy Bob Johnson had already met with an attorney and paid him $250 to start drafting articles of incorporation. The only thing that bothered Bobby was how much it was going to cost. According to the lawyer, he and Johnson would need to come up with at least a hundred thousand. Where they were going to get that kind of money he didn't know. Maybe if things worked out here, it would be okay. If not, he'd just have to keep trying.

The good thing was he and Bob Johnson had always gotten along. Fact is, he wished it were Johnson here with him now. He was smooth. Jack was good and tough but strange. When they'd gotten together in Houston, Jack had told him he'd been living in his car for five or six days, afraid of getting caught and so not checking into a hotel or motel.

THIRTY-FIVE

They decided to target an assistant manager of a Wells Fargo branch downtown. Not only did his bank look prosperous, but the man lived in an affluent area of town off American River Drive. For the rest of the week, Bobby and Jack shadowed him, following at a distance as he drove to work and back, logging times and travel routes.

On several occasions, Bobby cased the bank. And then he and Jack began to formulate a plan. They knew the manager had a wife and three children, and that the wife usually spent the day at home with a boy too young yet for school. They had also observed that she had her own car.

They decided that Jack would let Bobby off at the house, and he'd go in and take the woman and boy hostage. In the meantime, Jack would go to the bank and ask to see the manager. Once they had some privacy, he'd tell him Bobby was at his house and so he'd better do as Jack said. Jack might even let the man call home to verify what Jack had told him.

When the man gave Jack the money he demanded, he'd call Bobby who'd take the wife's car. They'd meet at a certain corner where Jack would pick him up. It sounded easy, and they could think of little that could go wrong. To make it look good, Jack would buy a suit so the manager would agree to see him. They'd steal a car, which Jack would use, and leave the Pontiac back at the apartment. When it was all over, they'd dump the stolen car and retrieve the one they'd bought.

When they went to Southgate Mall to buy Jack's suit, Bobby noticed an armored truck making a money pickup.

He nudged Jack. "Hey, man, look at that."

"You're not thinking of hitting it, are you?"

"Maybe. Let's just watch."

They sat in the car as two uniformed guards visited several businesses. At each store, one of the guards entered and came out within seconds with large sacks of currency. They took turns waiting in the truck. After stops at most of the stores the truck pulled out of the lot and crossed over the freeway. Bobby and Jack followed.

At the Florin shopping center, the men repeated similar activities. Then within half an hour, the truck again pulled into traffic and proceeded to a Bank of America two miles distant.

"Partner, we could do it," Bobby said. "We could either just hold up the truck, or steal it and the uniforms and make our own collections."

"No way Bobby. You were watching that truck the whole time. I was looking at other things. Cops. There were sixteen cop cars went by. Too damned many."

Thirty-Six

Back in 1962, Bobby, who was still in the Marines, was hanging around in San Francisco waiting for his buddy Ron Bates to receive a dishonorable discharge. As soon as he did, the two of them stole a car and took off. They had no plans other than to keep on driving till they reached someplace they liked. They agreed that in the event they were caught, the one who was driving would take the bust.

Bates had an aunt and uncle in Ohio and wanted to stop and see them. Bobby was tooling along, going west out of Columbus, when he heard a siren. Looking in his rearview mirror, he saw a cop car with flashing lights. He thought of running but didn't see much point in it. He was in unfamiliar territory and didn't know where he'd run to anyhow.

Bobby turned to Ron. "We're in deep shit, buddy. I guess you know that, huh?"

"You're the one who's in deep shit, man. I'm just along for the ride."

Bobby was tried and sentenced to two years for auto theft and interstate transportation of a stolen motor vehicle. He was given probation and a bad conduct discharge from the Marines. Ron walked free.

Back in Ponca City, he was feeling kind of down, not knowing where his life was headed, and decided to call Joan Hanks, a girl he'd dated now and then in high school, and see if she was dating anyone else. If she wasn't, he'd ask her out. She asked him to drop over.

Before long, he found a temporary job installing draperies for a furniture store. Lousy pay, less than $200 a month, but in Ponca City you took what you could get. After a few months, he talked things over with Joan, who by now had become his steady girl, and decided to move to Oklahoma City. Once there he answered an ad for "a sharp young man" to move into management. First, however, he had to sell encyclopedias door to door, which, like his last job, proved to be less than fulfilling.

One day when he was checking in after finishing his route, a co-worker named Jim Travis Ward said he knew how to make some easy money. Bobby was staying in a rooming house and invited Ward home with him. He led him up to his room and offered him the chair in the corner.

"So what's this about?" Bobby asked sitting on the edge of his unmade bed as Ward sat in an easy chair.

"Promise you'll keep it confidential."

"Sure."

"You won't tell anyone, not even that girl of yours you keep talking about."

"She doesn't need to know my business."

"This buddy and I been holding up a few service stations." He looked at Bobby. "Does that surprise you?"

"Takes a lot to surprise me, Ward."

"Man of the world, are you?"

Bobby chuckled. "Wouldn't go so far as to say that. But I've been around."

"So what do you think?"

"What do I think about what?"

"Robbing service stations."

"I'm waiting to be convinced."

Ward jumped up and strode to the window. Outside, the sun bounced through limbs of a big old maple tree before landing on the concrete sidewalk. He turned back to Bobby. "It can get you pumped up. Know what I mean?"

"Ain't got no experience to fall back on in that regard," Bobby answered. "What's your average take?"

"Hundred bucks maybe. Split between the two of us. Multiply that by two or three, and it ain't bad for a few minutes work."

"You done this a lot, Ward?"

"Enough! You go in there, show them your gun—don't even need to pull it on them. Man, they piss all over themselves trying to get you the cash quick as they can."

"You plan this out? The ones to hit. Or you just take it at random."

Ward laughed. "Like impulse buying, you mean?" He shook his head. "Naw, it ain't nothing like that. We check 'em out first. Hit only the big places, the chains. Hell, I don't want to hurt no little guys. Men who can't afford it. But them big oil companies. Shit, they're not going to miss a few hundred bucks now and then."

"Rich bastards are trying to take it all anyhow. Stealing all the business, suckering the average joe into thinking just cause they're big, they're better."

"You got it, man. So what do you say?"

"Sounds good."

"You want in?"

"I got to think about this some. It isn't something you jump right into, like maybe selling encyclopedias door to door."

"You ain't just a-shittin' me, man!"

"So you and this other man...."

"Buddy from high school. Name of Jim Bob Wilkes."

"Yeah, so you say you and Wilkes have been doing this for a time now?"

"A time, yeah. I mean we ain't no Jesse James or nothin' like that. But we do just fine. All you do is make up your mind you can do it. Keep your cool. Nobody's expecting anything. Nobody knows where we're going to hit. What I'm saying, there's no sense worrying about the law 'cause the law ain't going to be there. And we're in and out in less than a couple of minutes. Got our car parked around the corner, and off we go. No way to catch us; no way to trace us or know who we are."

"I think you convinced me, man."

"Hey, good deal, buddy." He squinted at Bobby. "You sure about this now?"

"Just gotta get me a gun, right?"

"No problem there. My daddy's got so many damned weapons you'd think he was getting ready to start a revolution. He ain't gonna miss any, especially if we don't take it permanent."

"So what's the next step?"

"Well, I've been thinking about this market, see? This Stop-and-Shop. I figure pickings might even be better there than at one of the gas stations. And it's one of them franchises, so we ain't hurting no one but some damn big company."

They hit their first market two days later. Ward did the talking while Bobby stood guard at the door to keep out any more customers. Everything went smoothly, and Bobby decided Ward was right. It got the old adrenaline going. Got a guy so high it took hours for him to come down. Better than any drug, Bobby thought, though he really wasn't experienced with drugs.

They tried a few more markets in town and decided to widen their area of operations. They moved into Texas, Kansas, Missouri and Arkansas—thirty or forty markets, all big chains. Bobby lost track of the count. He and Ward were flying high; no money problems now.

In the meantime he kept on seeing Joan. The families became acquainted and found they had a lot in common. Joan's folks seemed to cotton to him, and he could tell his daddy and mama liked Joan. "Like a daughter to me," Bobby's mama said. "Treats me better than you ever did."

"Now, Mama," Floyd said, "Bobby's a good boy. You know he is. Got himself into a little trouble now and then. But he's straightened out."

They were at the Davises' house. It was Sunday afternoon. The TV set was blaring, but no one was paying attention.

"So what are your intentions, son?"

"I don't know what you mean." Bobby knew all right, but it was making him as uncomfortable as hell. He liked Joan all right, maybe even loved her for all he could tell. But he didn't know if he was quite ready yet to settle down into marriage. It wasn't like up north or out there in California where getting hitched hardly meant a damned thing. In Bobby's part of the country, folks took it doggone seriously, the one institution held sacred above all others.

"Toward this young lady is what I mean."

"Now, Floyd," Bobby's mama said, "don't go trying to push these young folks into something for which they're not ready." She was sitting in the mohair easy chair by the front window. Bobby and Joan sat side-by-side on the matching sofa. Floyd was in his hickory rocker. "But if you've a mind to think about it, I wouldn't be against it myself."

"For gosh sakes," Bobby replied. "For gosh darn sakes!"

The thing was Joan's folks were dropping hints too. And they were as subtle about it as Bobby's folks. So with some reservations, they set the date, August 31, 1963.

When Bobby went back to Oklahoma City ostensibly to his job at which he'd told Joan he'd now been promoted, he called Ward to tell him that he and Joan were going to settle down. It was Monday afternoon. Bobby was tired from the drive back. He and Joan had been to the late show at the movie theatre the night before. He lay on his back on top of the patchwork quilt, the receiver to his ear.

"The thing is, old buddy," he told Ward, "I'm thinking of quitting all this."

"You too?" Ward said.

"You mean you're getting out?"

"Yeah."

"And you didn't tell me."

"It wasn't for sure, man. I'd have told you if it'd been for sure."

"Hey, Ward, I'm not mad about this. The opposite, really. I'm kind of relieved." Their last job had been a big supermarket in Topeka, Kansas, and they'd gotten out with eight thousand dollars.

"Me, too. I got the kids, you know, and my wife. Be nice to spend some time with them. And we certainly ain't got no money worries, at least for the time being. What about you?"

Ward was only a few years older than Bobby and had five kids. Bobby'd have to think about having even one! He wasn't at all sure he wanted to be that tied down.

"Try to find me a good job, I suppose," Bobby said. "But like you I'm in no big hurry."

"Okay, buddy," Ward said. "See you around."

• • •

The ceremony was a small one with family, close relatives and a few friends. Bobby and Joan moved into an apartment a couple blocks from her family's big old three-story house. And Bobby tried hard. Tried to settle into domestic life. But he wasn't sure it was going to work.

Thirty-Seven

Joan thought Bobby still worked for Collier's Encyclopedia, and he led her to believe that he did. He still traveled a few days a week, mostly looking for another job but simply screwing around wasting time too so she wouldn't get suspicious.

He really did want to get a job, but something good, something equal to his abilities. The money from the holdups was fine, but he was glad that part of his life was past. You could tempt fate only so far. And no matter what Ward said, sooner or later the authorities were going to catch up. For the time being Bobby was content. He still had plenty of money, and the marriage, despite his doubts, seemed to be working fine.

Then out of the blue he got a call at the rooming house from Jim Ward. "What you think about reconnecting and pulling a few more jobs?"

"Hey, man, I'm serious about not wanting to do this anymore."

"I know, I know. Me too. But I can't find no job. And I'm running out of money already."

"Running out of money?"

"Hey, you ain't got five kids to feed. What do you say?"

"Come on, man, it was good while it lasted, but it's over."

"A supermarket or two, that's all I'm asking. It's worth it, man."

"Tell you what, Ward. I'll lend you a thousand. Would that help?"

"I didn't call you to ask for money."

"I know, but I'm offering."

"You sure you won't—"

"I'm sure. So listen, how about we go out for a couple of beers, and I'll give you the money? Pay me back when you can. I trust you, Ward."

"You're sure as hell the first one who ever did."

For a few more weeks, it was okay. Then Ward called him again. "Hey, Bobby," he said. "Got my cousin up here from Georgia. Says he knows what he calls the perfect score, a small bank down there in Temple. Small community, three textile mills so the bank carries lots of cash to meet payroll every Friday."

"I'm telling you, Ward, I'm finished."

"Just listen to me. That very same bank was hit about five months back. Let me tell you what the haul was."

"Go ahead and tell me, but it isn't going to change things."

"Fifty thousand dollars. That's twenty-five thousand each, Bobby."

"You getting into that kind of thing, that's big trouble, man. That's a federal offense. You're going to get the FBI involved and who knows what all."

"It's going to be a real easy score. You wait and see."

"Fifty thousand, you say."

"Damned right that's what I say. So come on. Do I detect a little bit of weakening of your resolve?"

"Could might be."

"Could might! Hell, Bobby, it's a damned sure thing."

"So why isn't your cousin in on this then?"

"He ain't the type. He talks a good game is all. Come on, Bobby, what do you say?"

"All right, man, let's do it."

In mid-November the two of them flew to Atlanta, carefully checking their guns through baggage that couldn't be traced. Ward had called a brother-in-law who had no reason to suspect his motives and asked him to rent Ward and Bobby a car.

Next day they drove over to Temple and checked out the bank's location. They spent a couple of hours casing the place and planning not only a good escape route but an alternative route, as well. Then they stole another car in a nearby town. On the night of November 21, they hid the stolen car in the woods a short distance outside Temple. Next day, just before noon, they again went into the woods, left the rental car, and picked up the stolen car to be used in the robbery.

They used the same plan that had worked for them throughout. Bobby stood at the door while Ward did the talking. The bank was small, just two tellers cages and a desk for the manager. Even so, Bobby had to watch the three bank employees inside and look for potential customers outside. They figured it was early enough so no one would be cashing a check, but late enough so there'd be plenty of cash on hand. Since it was noon in a small town, folks would be working, tending to their kids, or eating their dinner at home.

It went without a hitch. Bobby could see that the two tellers were scared out of their minds and the manager was pissed as hell. At the same time, he wasn't going to do anything about it.

The first surprise came when they counted the money and found it was $6,800. Not bad for a few hours work—counting all the planning and such—

but far from the anticipated fifty grand. The second surprise was far worse. The man who owned the property where Bobby and Ward had parked the stolen car had become suspicious when he saw nobody around. And the car did have Atlanta plates, a little unusual for the area. He called in the number to the local police, who discovered it was stolen. More than that, the property owner had seen another car parked there too and taken down its license. When the police called him back, he told them about the first car.

By this time, the robbery had taken place, and the FBI got involved. Agents traced the rental car through Ward's brother-in-law, who told them who'd been driving it. In the meantime, Bobby and Ward flew back to Oklahoma City, and Bobby immediately took off for his and Joan's apartment.

He'd no sooner walked into the house when he got a frantic call from Ward. "Get the hell out," Ward said. "The FBI is into our ass."

"What is it?" Joan asked.

"Rush business trip to Denver. Gotta leave right away."

"To Denver? Why to Denver?"

"Don't ask me, Joan, that's just what they said."

"I thought you were selling encyclopedias."

"That's what I'm doing."

"Then why—"

"For God's sake, woman, I don't have time to argue."

"I'm sorry."

"I want you to come along."

"To Denver?"

"Where the hell else?"

"You want me to come to Denver?"

"Start packing, will you? That is if you want to. Wouldn't it be nice to get away for a few days. We can spend some time together, seeing the sights."

They were packed and gone within the hour. When Bobby heard the news that John F. Kennedy had been assassinated, he knew the bank robbery was no longer news. He didn't have to worry that Joan would read about it in the newspapers or hear about it on TV.

In Denver they got a motel room.

"Honey," Joan said as she started unpacking, "is something the matter?"

"What do you mean?"

"I've never seen you so tense."

"Don't worry about it, okay?"

"But I do worry about it, Bobby."

She opened a suitcase and saw a pile of bills.

"What is this, Bobby? I don't understand. Where'd all this money come from?"

He decided to level with her. He looked her straight in the eye. "It's from a bank robbery, Joan. Me and another guy knocked off this bank down in Georgia."

She sat down hard on the bed. "You robbed a bank!"

"Along with this buddy of mine."

"My God, I don't believe this. I thought only people like... I don't know, Dillinger or somebody, did things like that. Robbed banks."

"Now I guess you know different."

She looked hurt and frightened, as if she didn't know him at all. "How long's this been going on?"

"What going on?"

"You know. Robberies, that kind of thing."

"First time I hit a bank."

"A bank?"

"Yeah?"

"Does that mean you're robbed other places?"

"Look, Joanie..." He sat beside her and took her hand in his. She seemed to be in shock. "It doesn't mean anything. I'm still the same guy."

She jerked her hand from his and ran to the far side of the room. "It does not. It certainly doesn't mean that at all. I can't believe this, Bobby."

"Come on, Joan. You gotta get control of yourself."

"Control. You say I gotta get control. You're the one who's out of control. Jesus Christ Almighty, this is hard to take. I'd like not to believe it, but the damned evidence is right there on the bed."

"There's nothing we can do about it now."

"Nothing we can do! Nothing we can do! So, all this time I was thinking you were out there selling encyclopedias, you were doing something entirely different."

"I sold encyclopedias."

"Oh, yeah, for how long. A day? Two days? A week?"

There was little he could do to calm her down. He left the room for a couple of hours hoping it would help. It did, in a way. He could tell she'd done some thinking, that she was no longer angry. But maybe this was worse. It was like they didn't even know each other, like they were just two people sharing a room.

Even this phase passed and resolved itself into disappointment and hurt. He hated to see that look in her eye, as if she'd been horribly abused by someone she trusted and loved. Shit! he thought. What the hell are we going to do now?

They stayed a couple of days in Denver and then went on to Albuquerque. Joan didn't want to go out anywhere, didn't want to be seen with him. He asked her if she was afraid they'd be arrested. She shook her head. "Just mistrustful is all," she said. "Just disappointed and mistrustful."

They were sleeping in separate beds now. One morning Joan got up and told him she couldn't take it anymore. "It's no good. I can't go on running and hiding. I want to go home."

Reluctantly, Bobby agreed.

They took a train to Newton, Kansas. He asked her to wait a day and then call her folks to come and get her. She agreed, and he took a train to Detroit. Once there, he bought a car and drove to San Francisco. A month later he drove home and turned himself in, a mistake he would soon regret.

Thirty-Eight

Walt had decided he was going to transfer to a motorcycle squad.

"It's better," he'd told Nicki. "You get an extra hundred a month, and they let you take the bike home, so we'll save money there. We can get rid of one of the cars. And living in the Bay Area, we'll be much closer to the folks in Merced."

Though he hadn't quite convinced Nicki the decision was the right one, he'd been saving money for motor boots, breeches and a leather jacket. With nearly two years on the job, he was getting enough seniority to ask for the transfer.

Thirty-Nine

Mike looked at his watch: 3:10 a.m. Only a couple of hours left, his favorite time of the shift.

Earlier, a man on a motorcycle had hit a deer and crashed. The accident had required follow up at Golden State Hospital. Mike hated hospitals—standing in the emergency room, watching blood being swabbed from gaping wounds, listening to victims cries amplified by the tile floors and the bare walls. At the scene of an accident, these sounds were muffled by outside noise and diminished by open space.

Rather than focusing his attention on the face with a tube running into the nose, Mike looked at the white stockings on the nurse's legs. He wondered why a pretty young girl would want to wear something that ugly. Glancing up, he saw the nurse smile. He didn't respond.

• • •

It was funny, Mike thought, but he and Skip had worked for several full months as partners, and they always found something to talk about. Sometimes they didn't talk, and that was okay too. Sometimes Mike thought of himself and Pence as predators searching for a kill. Like a shark, he envisioned, prowling silently back and forth, gracefully maneuvering through traffic, the eight-foot radio antenna cutting the air like the big fish's dorsal cut through water. The effect of the black and white vehicle on its fellow travelers was much the same. Increased awareness of the driving laws and a noticeable observance of caution.

FORTY

Just when everything seemed ready for them to pull the bank job in Sacramento, Jack skinned his forehead and nose diving into the swimming pool. Then he split his lip while practicing with the sawed-off shotgun.

"Damn thing kicks like a mule," Jack said.

They were up in the foothills east of Sacramento, fussing around, knowing that there was no point in even thinking about all that money waiting in the bank.

"What do you expect with a six-inch stock and a ten-inch barrel? Jesus Christ Almighty, man, it'd be funny as hell if it weren't so serious."

"What do you think's so fucking funny?"

"You, Jack. You gotta admit you're a hell of a sight for a briefcase toting businessman."

To Bobby's surprise, Jack laughed. "Hell, Bobby, businessmen have accidents too."

"You don't mean you're wanting to go through with this?"

"Naw. It'd be just like saying to the feds, 'This is what I look like, come on and get me.'"

They could have changed roles, Bobby thought. But he wasn't at all comfortable with Jack holding the hostages.

As a consequence, they told Mrs. Sammas they'd located a place to bring their wives and were checking out. She said she was sorry to see them go and asked where she could send the cleaning deposit if it wasn't all used up.

"That's all right, Mrs. Sammas," Bobby said, "you just keep it now, you hear."

They loaded up the car and headed down U.S. 99 on what Bobby considered had to be one of the most boring trips he could take. Like Texas, miles and miles of nothing but miles and miles. He thought back to the first time he'd taken the very same trip, back in 1964 when he'd been dumb enough to go back to Oklahoma.

FORTY-ONE

After robbing the bank in Georgia and driving back to Oklahoma to turn himself in, Bobby thought he must have been crazy to ever think he might get probation. Instead, he'd been sentenced to the El Reno Correctional Institute. Right there in Oklahoma; home sweet home.

He'd been in El Reno only a month when Joan showed up with another man and announced she was getting a divorce. It made Bobby pissed as hell and indirectly led to further problems with the prison system.

Getting a divorce, was she? he thought. Not if he could help it. But the only damned way to do anything about it was to get the hell out.

He and a fellow inmate, a man named Louis Rondau, had discovered that an acetylene torch was stored in a small unlocked room. The locked outer door to the room opened up on an unguarded passageway which led to the perimeter fence. From there it led over the fence and out. All a person needed was a few minutes to cut the lock on the outer door. This was where the torch came in handy.

The two of them decided that they'd slip into the room individually, cut the lock, and hide in the passageway till it was dusk. They'd hit the fence just before lockup and count.

Bobby realized the plan wasn't perfect, but if all went right, it could work. Bobby and Rondau had waited for the call to clear the yard and then moved into the room. It was already getting dark, but not enough so they couldn't help see that the welding equipment was gone.

"Son-of-a bitch!" Bobby said. "Now what the hell are we going to do?"

Rondau didn't have time to answer before a prison workman walked into the room. Not a guard, but a "freeman" maintenance worker.

Bobby had snatched up a piece of pipe and threatened the man if he cried out. Actually, he felt like breaking open the fucker's head. He'd damn well do it too if the guy made a peep. Next, he and Rondau had alternated hitting and prying on the metal door that separated them from freedom. The damned thing wouldn't give. They knew that soon the evening meal would be ending. Then would come lock-up and head count. It wouldn't take long to see the two men were out of their cells, and then there'd be a general alarm.

"You got a problem here," the man they were holding captive said.

"No shit, fuckhead!" Rondau answered.

"No call to get nasty," the man told him.

"I'll be the judge of that," Rondau said.

"You'll get yourself in a peck of trouble you try anything else. What I'm saying is you turn yourselves in, about the only thing you're going to be charged with is unauthorized behavior. A hell of a lot less serious than it could be. Just being in a place where you're not supposed to be."

"We ain't going to get out anyhow, Bobby. What do you say?" Rondau asked.

"I guess," Bobby said.

"Look, fellas, you ain't even missed a count yet. So what's the worst could happen? A couple days in solitary and loss of privilege?"

"I think he's got a point," Rondau said.

Bobby agreed, and for the second time in a year he made a dumb mistake in taking advice and attempting to predict the behavior of federal authorities.

He was charged with attempted escape. And his waving a pipe at the civilian employee constituted assault on a federal officer. For each charge, an additional year was added to his twelve-year sentence. And being identified as an escape risk and hard-to-control inmate, he was transferred to Leavenworth. At twenty-one years and one month he was the youngest person ever to do time there.

FORTY-TWO

When Bobby first arrived at Leavenworth, he felt, for the first time ever, that he was a loser and most likely would be one all his life. On his first day there, an old con, a guy he'd hardly even noticed, came up to him in the mess hall. "You know, buddy, your spirits are so low, you have to look up at everyone. A piece of advice from a man who knows. You stay like that and you're finished."

Bobby realized the man was right and he'd have to do something about it. The huge forty-foot walls around the place confined nearly two thousand of the nation's worst offenders with a murder rate higher than that of most large cities. Leavenworth was where Bobby learned to be a con.

Prison sex accounted for most of the violence, and Bobby quickly learned that a young inmate needed protection in order to survive sexual predators. The reason Bobby was able to survive in such an atmosphere could be summed up in two words: Jack Twining.

One afternoon in the exercise area, Jack dissuaded a big brute of a man who had designs on Bobby by parting his skull with a five pound free weight. Bobby didn't know why Jack stuck up for him that way, other than that they both were in for bank robbery and that gave them something in common. They took to spending their time with each other whenever they could. This mostly meant exercising together in the yard.

Jack was a natural athlete. He was tough and con-wise.

"I knew you been in the joint before, Bobby," he said. "You got experience in being a con. But you haven't learned."

"What the hell you mean, I haven't learned?"

"Your attitude, man. I heard what that old con told you about being down so bad. And he's right. You gotta learn to view things differently."

"I'm listening."

"You worry about how long you're going to be here, about how many months or days till you're out, you're going to go crazy."

"You don't think about being on the outside?"

"I think about it. Wouldn't be human if I didn't. I'm talking about taking things day by day. Not taking 'em by the yard but taking 'em by the inch."

Bobby didn't believe him. The way he'd kept sane in the joint was to think of the time he was going to get out and becoming enraged if he thought that time was going to be increased by even a day or an hour. "How the fuck do you do that?" he asked

"By looking forward to movies on weekends, special meals on holidays, the once-a-week change of the bed sheet. The bright spots."

• • •

Bobby had never met anyone like Jack. Even in total confinement, he was independent, like a cat, not needing nor caring for anybody or anything. Except in his friendship with Bobby, he was a loner, cold blooded.

He had the cagey smartness of an animal. He didn't know things, he understood them. He had the ability to marshal his entire energy toward the accomplishment of a task.

Even though it meant pulling easier time, Bobby had been sorry when in 1965 the U.S. Bureau of Prisons assigned him to a new penitentiary in Marion, Illinois, a maximum-security prison designed to replace Alcatraz.

On the day he arrived, he walked into one of the TV rooms just in time to see one inmate fatally stab another. A guard identified Bobby as a witness. Within the hour, he was collared and interrogated. Because he refused to tell what he'd seen, he got busted to solitary. Great fucking start! The God-damned hole on his very first day.

When Bobby got out of solitary two months later, a hunger strike was in progress protesting the shooting of an inmate by a guard. Prison authorities, attempting to crush the strike and unearth contraband foodstuffs, were checking cells unannounced. Unaware of the shakedowns, Bobby had hidden a scale drawing of a silencer in his bunk, a pencil drawing passed to him by a friend he knew from Leavenworth. Authorities found the drawing during the first cell search, and Bobby went back to solitary.

Three years later Bobby went back to Leavenworth, and after five months, he again returned to Marion. In July of 1969, Bobby was transferred to the Community Treatment Center in Houston. Three months later, he was paroled.

Forty-Three

Bobby found that being on parole wasn't all that easy. First off, he had a hell of a time finding a job. After what seemed like endless application forms and an interview here and there, he was hired to assemble orders in the shipping department at Texas Marine Industrial Supply Company. It wasn't much, not very challenging, but it kept the parole officer off his back.

Since he'd had two years of college in prison, he decided to enroll at the University of Texas in Houston. It didn't work out. He thought the college people were nuts, holding demonstrations against the very government that was paying their way and protesting a war he didn't give a shit about. Let 'em screw around shooting at each other, he thought, as long as it wasn't him over in Vietnam.

One day he had trouble with his phone bill, something about his not paying the damn connection charge or whatever, and he went in to straighten it out. That's where he met Carmel Garcia, and he felt right away she was something special. Tiny, with dark eyes and hair, she looked somehow vulnerable and lonely. They'd hit it off right away. Like pieces of a puzzle, each filling voids in the other, they fit, he thought. Before long they moved in together. And Bobby thought he was all ready to square up. No more crime or messing around. Then Carmel got pregnant. And even though he was supposed to get a raise, it didn't come through.

Up till now he'd been vaguely aware of the armored cars that drove around all over Houston. Now he paid attention, following them sometimes, watching what the guards did and how they handled the money they collected. Careless for the most part, he noted. But hell, who could blame them? It was someone else's money, not theirs, so why should they give a shit? The idea of hitting an armored car appealed to him. That would be a score! Just like the Brink's guys had done back in Boston.

It wasn't long before Carmel began to pressure him to get married. She knew she'd be in trouble with the phone company once they found out she was pregnant and single. Besides, she wanted maternity benefits, and she probably wouldn't get them if the baby was illegitimate.

As her pregnancy advanced, Carmel became more dependent and more despondent, harder and harder to get along with. Bobby didn't think he was getting tired of her, but something was wrong. Maybe it was just plain boredom. Even so, he cared about her, and so on March 16 they were married.

Despite having little money and no good solution in sight, a part of him still cared enough to want to go straight. He felt he had potential and promise. He was bright. All he needed was a break. He made contact with a former prison buddy, Bob Johnson, and they talked about starting a nursing home. Both had learned basic nursing skills at Marion. They contacted an attorney. The bubble burst when the attorney told them how much money the venture would take.

Bobby went back to shadowing armored cars and then received the call from Jack.

FORTY-FOUR

They were sitting in the patrol car watching for speeders. Funny, Roger thought, how much he and Walt depended on each other and how close they'd become. Probably because each knew his partner's life was in his hands. Even their families had become close spending evenings and days off with each other.

He glanced at Walt. "You trust me, don't you?" he asked.

"Do I trust you?"

"Uh huh."

"Yeah, I trust you."

It was April 1, 1970. Roger and Walt, working the graveyard shift, were beginning their twentieth month on the Highway Patrol. Partners, working Beat 8—Highway 99 from the Ventura turnoff at Castaic Junction, north to the top of the five-mile grade.

FORTY-FIVE

Bobby and Jack had left the Sacramento Valley and were driving down toward Los Angeles. As they crossed the ridge of the Tehachapis, Bobby noticed a lot of construction on both sides of the highway.

"With all this going on, they have got to be blasting to get through these hills!" Jack said.

"You're darned right," Bobby replied, "and blasting means explosives. So if we ever decide we need some, we sure know where to get them."

"Where the hell are we anyhow?"

"Someplace between Bakersfield and L. A. I think the last town was Gorman and the next is Newhall, or something. According to the signs, L. A. is thirty or forty miles farther."

Jack dozed as Bobby guided the Pontiac south on the Golden State Freeway. It was evening, most traffic headed out of the city. They stopped at a Motel 6 in Long Beach and went looking for apartments. They found one on Ximino Street. The manager filled out the rental agreement and warned Bobby and Jack against excessive noise and furniture damage. He told them that each apartment was inspected weekly for cleanliness.

• • •

"Did you hear what that dipshit said about checking the place every week?" Bobby said.

"I heard."

"Hell, that means we're gonna have to take all the guns with us all the time. If we leave them here, that fucker will come nosing around and see them."

"I'd feel much better anyhow with keeping them in the car."

"Jesus Christ, how many guns do we need to make you happy? One apiece should be enough far as I'm concerned."

"You never know. The more, the merrier, I always say."

"How many are there?"

Jack counted on his fingers: "A .44 mag carbine I stole from Talbert. Your sawed-off 12 gauge, the two two-inch .38's, the four-inch .357 magnum from the Texas Highway Patrol that you bought in Houston, and the three .45 automatics I picked up in St. Louis. I guess that's it."

"You forgot the 9 MM Browning."

"All right. That's seven pistols, a rifle and a shotgun. I don't think that's too many."

"Not if you're planning to start a fucking war!" Bobby grinned. "Anyhow, let's get to work. I'm gonna hit the library and try to get the bank officials located like we did up north. I'll let you out up in Hollywood somewhere. Stop at one of those actors' supply shops or costume places and try and get some makeup and stuff for disguises. You can use it to cover your scabs. And get some walkie talkies. We may want to use them to stay in touch on the job."

FORTY-SIX

A flickering of stars was visible through a haze lying over the city as Bobby and Jack left the apartment and drove to a nearby diner.

"Sambo's! Sounds like a jig joint," Jack said as they pulled into the lot.

Bobby ignored him, recognizing the resurgence of one of his ugly moods, the kind that never lay far below the surface.

"Did you hear me? I don't want to be eatin' with a bunch of hams!"

"Jack, dammit, take it easy. It's a goddamned pancake house. A chain restaurant."

As they entered, Bobby looked quickly around and was relieved to see there were no Negroes in view. Hell, he didn't like them either. What prejudice you didn't get from being raised in the South, you quickly acquired in prison. But Jack was different. He hated blacks with more than a passion. And when Jack got into one of these moods, he did crazy things. On the train, he had refused to eat one meal because the waiter had been colored. Bobby relaxed even more when he noted that the help was all white. He had half finished his meal when he suddenly saw Jack stiffen and begin to reach for his waistband.

"Look at that, Bobby! A ham and a white gal! I'm going to kill 'em both!"

"Jesus Christ, Jack! What the hell's wrong with you? You want to send us back to the joint over trash like that? It isn't worth it. Sit down and take it easy and pull your coat back down!"

"Fuck it, Bobby, I'm not staying in here with that nigger and nigger lover! I'll wait in the car." Twining quickly pulled his sweatshirt back over the grip of the .45 and stalked from the cafe. The newly arrived couple either didn't notice or ignored his glare as he passed near their booth.

When Davis returned to the car, he found Twining dry-firing a four inch .357 magnum pistol at the pair in the restaurant.

"Are you crazy, or what?" he exploded. "You want us to get busted for some stupid thing, don't you? Well, I've had it. No more. We go back and split up. I'm not gonna take a fall just 'cause you want to act stupid!"

Jack swung around the .357 to point it in Bobby's direction. "Now just one fucking minute. We're partners, damn it, and don't you forget it."

"Partners, shit!" Bobby yelled, jumping from the car. "I don't want nothing to do with a crazy man." He kept on walking, knowing that if the gun Jack was holding was loaded, he'd probably get shot. He wasn't surprised when he heard the hammer click on the empty cylinder. That bastard really *is* crazy, he thought, as he walked back toward the apartment.

When he was about a block away, he thought he heard the Pontiac start up and squeal out of the lot. He didn't look back.

He let himself in and went straight for his bedroom where he stretched out on the bed. He finished a smoke but didn't remember dozing. He was suddenly aware that Jack was standing above him. He looked somehow calmer but still wore the .45 automatic tucked into his belt.

"Hey, man," he said, "I just want to know if you were serious about us breakin' up. I mean, you really got no right to be feeling that way. Nothin' happened."

"What time is it? Where the hell you been?" Bobby could see by the watch on Jack's left wrist that it was after midnight. They had left the diner three hours earlier.

"Just driven' around. Cooling it, really. Right after you left, I thought I'd wait for that pair, but they never came out. I saw two of them spooks up on the freeway in an old pickup. Smart asses. One of them gave me the finger when I pulled up alongside. The passenger window was up in the Pontiac, and I didn't want to shoot through it, else I'd have blown 'em away. By the time I fell back behind and came up on their right, they took an exit. If I could have slowed in time, I'd have backed up and chased them. But a Highway Patrol car came along just then."

"Don't you see, Jack?" Bobby was seething. "That's the crap I'm talking about. Dammit, you're smarter than that. If we got to take chances, let's make them worthwhile. Like a hit! There's no payoff to screwing around with some hams. It's an easy way back to the joint is all. We got to hang loose and make the big score!"

"You're right, Bobby. It's just that sometimes these things get the best of me. I'm not built to take shit from anybody. You know that. And when somebody, some jig especially, gives me a ration, I'm gonna fix his ass."

"Okay. It's over and done. Let's get some sleep and get going on something tomorrow."

Bobby knew his troubles with Jack were far from over.

FORTY-SEVEN

Bobby and Jack were driving back to the apartment the next day when they fell in behind an armored truck on the Santa Monica Freeway. They were returning from the downtown library where they'd been gathering the names of bank officials as they'd done in Sacramento. Acting on impulse, Bobby followed the truck. It was bound for the Santa Anita racetrack. Bobby pulled off to the right and watched as it pulled through the fenced security gate.

"Bet that sucker's just loaded with cash," he remarked. "Change for all the two-dollar windows. Probably a hundred grand."

"Well, if it's taking in a hundred grand for change, you can imagine how much it will bring out after the races," Jack said as he squinted into the bright April sunshine.

"Hey, that's right," Bobby said, his excitement mounting. "Let's hang around and see if they do haul the money out in an armored car. If so, we can just as well toss the list of bank big shots. This'd be a much better score. Besides, with an armored car, we can pick our own place and time."

Fifteen minutes later the truck rolled back out to the street. Again Bobby followed along behind. The truck drove on surface streets for a dozen blocks and then pulled into a MacDonald's restaurant. Two uniformed guards got out, locked the doors and disappeared inside.

"I'll go in and see where they sit and if they order anything to go," Bobby said. "There might be another guard in the truck. You wait till I give you the sign and see if you can get a look inside. Check for weapons, radio, inside hood latch, anything that we might need to know."

"And you look and see what kind of fire power they wear on their hips."

• • •

The place was crowded, but Bobby managed to get into line next to the guards. He waited till the men placed their orders. Then he walked to the door and gave a casual wave to Jack still seated in the Pontiac. He positioned himself where he could observe both the guards and their vehicle. Good! They were sitting down inside to eat.

Bobby watched as Jack approached the armored truck and began peering inside. Shit, thought Davis, no matter what he does, he has the look of a crook about him. He'd been so cool in the joint. A guy who could play any game, who could really con. Now he couldn't do a simple thing on the outside. Bobby continued to marvel on this as Jack glanced furtively around. To anyone watching, he'd surely give the impression that he was about to swipe the hubcaps or siphon gas. Fortunately, his check took less than a minute, and he returned to the Pontiac. Bobby went out to join him.

"Well?" Bobby asked.

"It's got a radio of some type. No guns visible, but mounted behind the seat is a box that looks like it might contain long guns. Rifles, shotguns, maybe even a machine gun. The windows are bulletproof glass. There are holes where they can shoot out, to the sides and rear, nothing to the front. You can't get to the engine from the outside, but the tires are standard pneumatic. We could take it out that way."

"How about another man?"

"Nope. Only the two."

"Anything else?"

"Yeah. There was a daily schedule of pickups and deliveries on the dashboard. It shows they go back to Santa Anita at 4:45 and then to a bank. They have a couple of other pickups between now and then."

"Now we're clicking. We'll leave and try to meet them at 4:45 at the track. Then we'll follow and see what they do with the money!"

• • •

According to plan, the red Pontiac was positioned near the entrance to the race track parking lot at 4:30 p.m. A minute later the now-familiar armored truck rolled by again entering the security area where it parked. One man got out, walked to the building and disappeared inside. In a minute or two he was back with three additional uniformed guards. The four made two trips each between the vehicle and the building. Each carried two metal boxes.

Once loaded, the truck took off with Bobby driving the Pontiac in its wake. Almost immediately, Bobby shouted, "This is it! Right here on the ramp! They can't see us from the freeway. Even if the guards put out a call, with this evening rush traffic, the cops couldn't get to us. What we have to do is disable the thing right here."

"We can do that by blocking the road and maybe shooting the tires. But how do we get inside?"

"We blow the fucking thing wide open with dynamite!"

"Sounds good. How do we make sure it can't move, that it's totally disabled?"

"Wait a minute, let me think. How about this? What if we shoot and kill the bastards right in the truck. Then it wouldn't go nowhere."

"But I told you the glass is bulletproof."

"Shit, nothing is bulletproof enough to stop a .50 caliber machine gun round. The armor piercing stuff can go through the sides of a tank. We can get a .50. When I was stationed at Pendleton, they had .50's mounted on half-tracks, and they weren't even guarded."

Getting more excited by the minute, the two men began to flesh out the plan en route to the apartment.

"Hey, how's about this?" Jack suggested. "We can take a pickup truck and put the .50 in the back, stop on the ramp right in front of the armored car and blast them. Then blow it open and make it."

"Yeah, except we ought to get something bigger than a pickup. We'll steal a dump truck. That way, the ramp will be totally blocked. We can put the car a block or so away and split to it on foot. What do you say?"

Twining leaned back and closed his eyes, "Okay. It sounds okay. We'll wait till a week from today, next Friday. Between now and then, we got to find some explosives, steal the machine gun and the dump truck."

"Also, we ought to follow the trucks a couple more times just to make sure that the time and place is right. Tomorrow, we'll run down to Pendleton and see about our chances of getting a machine gun. There are always a lot of visitors on Saturday, and we should be able to get onto the base with no problem. Then, if that looks good, we'll try for explosives. Maybe we can get those there too."

"If not, we can go back up the freeway. Remember those construction zones in the mountains just before we hit L. A.?"

"It's settled then. Shake, partner, this will be a big one. Maybe up to a half a million."

• • •

The following day was bright and clear. The Santa Ana winds were blowing, moving away most of the smog.

Bobby told the M.P. at the gate that they were there to visit his brother who was in training. They were given a visitor's pass. As Bobby had recalled, there were APC's sitting in long lines. Some of these, because they were used for range training, had .50 caliber machine guns mounted on them. The ammo dump was located where he remembered it. "There's where we'll get the ammo we need. We'll try for armor piercing."

They left by another gate, keeping the visitor pass, and made plans to return Monday or Tuesday evening.

That night they treated themselves to a movie at The Imperial Theater in Long Beach.

Forty-Eight

It had been a long and tiring day for Ivory Jack Tidwell. He and his wife Pamela had been to a family reunion at Lake Isabella sixty miles to the east of Bakersfield. At the end of a day of beer drinking, good food, and general relaxation, they'd stopped at his parents' home in Bakersfield for dessert and coffee. Pam was tired. She'd fallen asleep on the way up the north side of the ridge. Jack felt like sleeping too. But he had to go to work in the morning in Port Hueneme. The U.S. Navy frowned on absenteeism, and since a cruise to Japan was coming up in less than three weeks, he didn't want an Article 15 hanging over his head. It was already 11:15 as he drove the VW through Gorman. He figured they might make it home by one.

As he started down the grade on the L. A. side of the summit, he was taken by the beauty of the evening. It was chilly but clear, the moon and stars shining. Even in the steady flow of traffic heading back to the city, Jack felt a sense of peace and serenity.

A vehicle traveling in the opposite direction suddenly made a U-turn directly into his path. Jack braked and turned hard to his right. Even so, it was close.

"Damn! That guy must be crazy or drunk!"

"What's wrong?" his wife mumbled sleepily.

"That crazy driver right in front of us. When I get close enough, try and get his license number."

"All right." She pulled a notepad and pen from her purse.

"Can you read it? It's OSY 805, I think."

"Yes, OSY 805. I've got it." She held up the notepad for Jack to see.

"What is that anyhow?" he said. "A Buick? An Impala?"

"I don't know. They all look so much alike these days." Pamela leaned back against the seat and closed her eyes.

"Let me get closer." He accelerated and moved into the fast lane beside the other car. The driver, a lone male, glanced over at them.

"Roll down your window, honey," Jack said.

Both vehicles were now slowing down.

"If you promise not to do anything." She rolled down the window

The red vehicle pulled to the right shoulder and stopped. Jack pulled his Volkswagen alongside and shouted through his wife's open window, "You drive like hell! I've got a good mind to kick your ass! You hear? I ought to kick it good!"

The driver of the red car very deliberately pointed a two-inch revolver out his side window at the Tidwells. "Okay, punk. I want to see it happen!" he spit. "Get your ass out and do it!"

Jack stiffened in shock. "A gun. He's got a gun!"

"Please don't shoot. We didn't...." Pamela was interrupted by the approach of a car behind them.

Jack let out the clutch and gunned it.

"Jeez, that guy's crazy!" he breathed to Pam. "Let's find a phone and call the police.

As they headed down the mountain, Jack kept checking in the rearview mirror to see if the man with the gun was following. "No sign of him," he told Pam. "And we're almost off this damned hill."

"There!" she said. "Off to the left. A Union station. They're sure to have a phone."

He pulled off the highway at Violin Canyon road and drove to the phone booth in the corner of the station lot. "Give me that license number on it."

He looked up the phone number and dialed.

"California Highway Patrol."

"I want to report a guy with a gun!" Jack blurted and started to relate what had happened.

• • •

Jo Ann Tidey grabbed a pen. "Sir, you'll have to slow down and speak more clearly. You say that license number was OSY 805?"

"Yeah. A guy in a red car, a GM product I think."

While she was still copying down the details, Jo Ann Tidey swivelled her chair halfway around and punched the license number into the teleprinter which was connected to the huge Department of Motor Vehicles computer in Sacramento. She pushed the key which would request registration information on the vehicle at the same time depressing a second key. The latter would connect with the Autostatis computer at CHP headquarters and check for stolen or wanted information.

She reread the information given her, obtained the Tidwell's home address and assured the caller that all CHP units in the area would be alerted to the incident and they would try to apprehend the offender.

By the time she was off the telephone, both machines had responded with a printout to her terminal.

She learned that the license plate, OSY 805, had been issued to a 1964 Pontiac coupe, that it was currently registered, but that the ownership had been recently transferred. The new owner's information had not yet been entered into the system. She also knew that it had not been reported stolen, nor was it wanted for any other reason by any California law enforcement agency.

Such incidents occurred frequently in the Newhall Area, most likely because of the ready availability of guns. It was a hunting and plinking area which attracted shooters from the city. For the life of her, Jo Ann couldn't imagine why anyone would want to threaten another person with a gun or take pot shots at someone in another vehicle. Yet it happened all the time. Just a couple of months ago near Fresno to the north, two guys had shot it out with a .22 pistol and a .12 gauge shotgun because one accused the other of not lowering his high beams. By the time officers arrived, both men were wounded.

She turned to the radio to broadcast the BOLO, be on the lookout.

• • •

"Well, we did our part," Jack Tidwell said as he and his wife were once more on their way home. "The CHP has all the information. I guess they'll try and find him. With all these cars out here, though, I doubt that they will."

FORTY-NINE

Bobby and Jack had left the apartment that afternoon to come up and check out the tool sheds and small shacks they had spotted three days earlier. They'd arrived just before dark. It was an area of steep hills sparsely covered with oak trees and outcroppings of rocks. Bobby grinned to himself as he visualized Indians topping a rise in a long single line. Probably a whole bunch of cowboy movies had been made around here.

"Let's go check the place we saw the construction shacks," Jack said.

"Okay." The construction site was a half mile or so east of the highway. "But what about the car?"

"Just pull it off and park it."

"Hell no, the cops tow them away out here. Especially after dark."

"Tell you what, I'll go take a look. You drive around and wait. I'll take a radio and we can keep in touch. If I need anything, I'll call. If you see anybody from the highway, warn me."

"Fine. But take the earplug for the radio. That way, if there's a watchman or something, he won't hear me talking."

"Good idea." Jack peered through the windshield. "See that wide spot up ahead? Pull in there and let me out. I want to see if I can get the .44 mag unjammed."

"Hell no, are you crazy? You can't go walking around like that. Take the pistol. But don't go traipsing around with a fucking rifle."

"It just seems that if you're in this kind of country, you should be packing a rifle. Besides, it's damned dark out there."

"I'll call you if I see any injuns."

"Fuck you, too." Jack slid from the car and disappeared over the bank.

Bobby pulled back onto the road and turned on the walkie talkie. "Jack, can you hear me? Jack? Come in Jack. Do you read? Jack?" Nothing.

He pulled off to the side, rolled down his window and stuck out the antenna. Still nothing. Fuck, he thought. Guess next time we'll know to try the things out first.

What was he going to do now? He hated the damned waiting, not knowing if Jack was okay.

• • •

He had pulled off at a paved area behind a beat up car. Passengers looked like a family of Mexicans, one of whom was pouring gallon after gallon of water into the steaming radiator. He could tell that their seeing him sitting there watching had made the group uneasy. This in turn made Bobby uneasy.

Damn it. He didn't want to leave, but he'd have to. He'd try later to contact Jack. He turned around onto the highway which had no divider point and headed south. Either he had misjudged the distance or the driver of an approaching Volkswagen was just a hard ass. In any case, the VW pulled right behind him, honked and kept flashing the lights.

Davis slowed so it could pass. Instead of passing, the driver pulled alongside and hollered something.

Well, look at this shit, Bobby thought. Here I am with eight guns in my car and these two punks are going to try to take me! He pointed the gun at the one in the passenger side, and the car sped away.

"You son-of-a-bitch, I'd like to fix your ass!" he screamed at the disappearing taillights. He glanced into the outside mirror and pulled back onto the highway. Shit! He sure as hell would like to go after the punk. But Jack was still out in the hills someplace. He'd have to find him and then get back to town. He tried the walkie talkie again. Either the damn things were no good or Jack had turned his off. He drove south for another couple of miles and then turned around.

A short time later he spotted Jack standing on the shoulder of the road near where he'd let him out.

"Where the hell have you been?" Jack asked. "I've been calling on the radio for the last fifteen minutes."

"They just don't fucking work. Anyway, I think we might have trouble." Bobby explained what had happened.

"You have all the fun," Jack answered. "Should have blown them away."

"No man!" Bobby told him. "They were just a couple of kids. Let's just hope that they got a good scare and go on about their business."

Jack opened the door and got in. "Come on, we can probably catch up to them. This baby will outdo a damned VW."

"Let's don't push it, okay!" He steered back onto the road. "As a matter of fact, we should stash the damn guns."

"Where in the hell are we going to stash them! You know the fucking apartment manager."

"I'll do it, man. I'll let you out first. If I get busted, you can come bail me out."

"Are you nuts? We're both parole violators. If they catch you and print you, you'll go back to the joint. And there ain't no way I'm going to walk into a friggin' police station and try to get you out! Let's just head back to town. Probably nothin' will happen. Just drive normal and don't attract attention."

"I think we should ditch the guns."

"Not my guns, we ain't!"

Bobby suddenly spied what he thought was a cop car. "Jack, I think there's a cop behind us."

"Has he got the light on?"

"Nope!"

"Then just keep going." Jack checked the .45 in his belt and pulled another from under the seat.

"Here's a ramp. I'll pull off and see if he comes with us. He may go by."

"Nope, he's still on our tail. It looks like two of them in there."

"Well, we still don't know for sure if they made us."

"Make sure you stop at the stop sign, signal and everything."

Bobby pulled off at the exit marked "Henry Mayo Drive." He drove to the bottom of the off ramp, stopped as required, and turned right. Within a hundred yards was another stop sign at a T-intersection. On the right was a J's Restaurant and a Standard station to the north of it. Bobby turned right. Just before he got to the gas station, he saw the patrol car's red light come on.

He pulled into the driveway of the station and stopped.

"Stay in here, Jack, and let me handle it. I can probably talk us out of this!" He jumped from the car and started back toward the officers.

FIFTY

"That's it!" Roger told Walt.

"What?"

"The car they put out on the brandishing thing. Didn't she say a red '64 Pontiac, OSY something?"

Walt had been trying to fix his flashlight which wouldn't turn on. He laid it on the seat between them. "Let me look." He picked up the hot sheet on which he had scrawled the BOLO. "A '64 Pontiac, OSY 805. That's it!"

"Call it in. And maybe we better get a backup."

He picked up the mike. "Newhall, 78-8."

"Go ahead to Newhall, 78-8."

"Newhall, we're behind the red Pontiac now, OSY 805 southbound at the truck scales."

This was the only portion of Highway 99 that was full freeway in the Newhall area and so had overhead lighting. Roger could clearly see the vehicle they were pursuing. Bright red with a good polish with what looked like two people inside. No hippie markings, peace signs, or hot rod features. Nothing like dingle balls or excessive chrome, mud flaps or purple side lights.

"78-8, 78-12," the radio spoke.

Walt picked it up and answered, "Go ahead 12."

Alleyn's voice came through the speaker.

"Hey, we're coming north from Lyons. We'll give you a backup on the stop. We'll turn and wait at Valencia off. 10-4?"

"10-4!" Walt said. "We'll make the stop at Valencia!"

Roger could see beyond any doubt that there were two occupants in the vehicle. Both at one point had turned and looked back. "They sure as hell know we're back here," he said, "I wonder if they know why."

As the two vehicles passed the Castaic Inspection Facility, their speeds had dropped to between fifty-five and sixty.

"He's playing it cool," Walt said.

"Yeah, they made us as soon as we hit the freeway lights."

The Pontiac's right signal light came on.

"Uh oh. They're going off on Henry Mayo," Roger said. "Better let dispatch and 78-12 know."

Walt called dispatch.

The car pulled off the Henry Mayo ramp, made a full stop at the bottom and turned right. It proceeded the short distance to the intersection with the pre-freeway Highway 99. Again, the car made a legal stop and turned right.

Walt spoke into the microphone. "They're turning north on the old highway" The information would be picked up by both Newhall dispatch and 78-12, which was rolling to back them up.

At the northeast corner of Henry Mayo Drive and the old highway was a J's Restaurant and a Standard gas station.

"Light 'em up," Walt said.

As Roger reached for the red spot handle, the Pontiac turned into the driveway of the Standard station. It stopped in the driveway about thirty feet off the road.

"Making the stop at the Standard station by J's," Walt murmured into the mike.

Roger put on his hat, flipped the radio speaker to outside and climbed out.

"I'm going to take the shotgun," Walt said as he released the .12 gauge from the security of the Lectro-lock.

"I'll go up, you cover."

Since the area was well lighted, Roger left his flashlight in the car. Also, because it was a semi-high risk stop, he left his ticket book on the seat.

Because it was only a misdemeanor offense that had been reported, he didn't feel that the drawing of his sidearm was justified. Instead, he unhooked the safety strap of his swivel holster and held his hand on the butt of the revolver.

He approached cautiously along the left side of the vehicle, stopping before he reached the edge of the driver's door.

He could see that the rear deck and seat were clear. The driver's and passenger's hands were free and visible. No bad vibes so far. The car looked clean-cut, so did the occupants.

• • •

Walt had been surprised when the red Pontiac stopped in the service station driveway rather than pulling into the pump island or a little farther to a parking place near J's where it seemed to be headed. He placed his hat on his head and aimed the white spotlight into the rear window of the vehicle. He grabbed the pump action shotgun and stepped from the Dodge.

Two people in the car. The APB had given only a lone suspect, but that was the car, all right—OSY 805. Maybe the other guy had been sleeping or slouched down. Anyhow, you could rarely depend on witnesses to get things straight.

As Roger approached the driver's side, Walt moved to the right front of the patrol unit, a position from which he could see Roger and partially observe the actions of the occupants.

• • •

Roger had his hand on his gun. "Step out, please," he said.

"Yes, sir."

A slight southern accent? Young man. Caucasian. In his twenties. Conservatively dressed. Chino pants, yellow zipper jacket, clean shaven, short hair, youngish, innocent expression, if anything. Certainly not the criminal type.

"Step back here, please."

"What's this all about, officer?" the man asked but did as he was told.

"Turn around. Place your hands on the roof. Feet back and spread them."

Again the man complied.

Roger began a cursory search.

• • •

As Roger began the pat down, Walt moved two yards forward. He was between the two vehicles but to their right. He could see the back of the head of the passenger. Not a "long hair." The passenger started to get out of the car.

Walt brought the shotgun to port arms. "Hold it!" he shouted. It seemed kind of foolish—playing cops and robbers here in this gas station. People already were starting to stare. The man kept coming. Walt could see his face, the start of a mustache. Mean? Maybe. Maybe just awakened and upset.

"I said hold it!" he repeated, taking another step, the shotgun still at port arms. He could see that the guy was about thirty years old. He wore a green sweatshirt with a hood. Did he have something in his right hand? Oh, God, something was wrong. He was moving faster, coming out at a crouch.

"Get your hands up! Keep them there!" Walt yelled, feeling for the push safety on the shotgun.

The man raised his hands but only to his shoulder. The .357 magnum in his right hand fired twice. The first shot struck Walt under the left armpit, penetrated his left lung, the aorta and right lung, exiting from the right side of his back. The second slug, fired almost instantaneously, also entered below the left armpit. It perforated the right lung and lodged in the spine.

Walter Carroll Frago was dead before his body struck the asphalt.

• • •

As he was starting his frisk, Roger heard Walt's shouts. He glanced toward the far side of the car. The man he was searching moved to his left as if to give him a better field of vision.

Two shots rang out.

Roger saw Walt stumble and begin to fall.

Instinctively, he drew his revolver. He knew that the danger must be coming from the passenger. Jesus Christ Almighty! The passenger had a revolver. He was firing it at Roger. Roger pointed his gun at the man in the green sweatshirt and squeezed the trigger.

In the meantime, the driver had stepped back from the car. He drew a two-inch Smith and Wesson Chief's Special revolver from his shirt.

Roger was surprised by the pain he felt in his side. He looked toward the young man only two feet away. The man fired again at point blank range.

Roger David Gore did not die immediately. The two .38 caliber rounds penetrated his chest, one lodging in the spine and the other exploding in his spleen.

• • •

Skip Pence and Mike Alleyn, operating Unit 78-12, overheard the conversation between 78-8 and Newhall dispatch. They had just cleared a stop in the Newhall township area on a vehicle with no taillights.

"Let's go get in on this," Skip said. "We'll back them up."

Skip called Roger and Walt car-to-car and told them his and Mike's locations. He said they'd come and assist at the Valencia off-ramp. He positioned the unit on the Valencia southbound onramp so that they could view southbound traffic and backup 78-8. They knew that Frago and Gore wouldn't make the stop until they were in position.

Within seconds, they heard the call that the suspect vehicle was leaving the freeway at Henry Mayo Drive, approximately one mile north of their position. Skip grabbed the mike and advised that they'd be there in a minute.

They sped down the ramp and made a quick U-turn through the divider. While racing northbound at well over a hundred miles an hour, Skip heard Frago advise that they were making the stop at the Standard station near J's. As the patrol car bounced over the bumpy highway, he had fleeting thoughts about what the sergeant would say if they crashed while running without red light and siren, particularly since this was only to provide backup on a suspected misdemeanor. What the hell, he thought, it's worth it just to get in on the action. He floored the accelerator.

Unit 78-12 took the Henry Mayo off ramp at a speed in excess of 75 miles per hour. Skip grinned as he saw Mike clinging to the shotgun as they turned left at the bottom of the ramp, the patrol car in a semi-controlled broadside skid.

Skip slowed to fifty while turning right off Henry Mayo Drive onto north-bound Old Highway 99. There they were, right in the entrance to the Standard station. Skip could see the red Pontiac which had come out on the BOLO and the easily recognizable black and white unit. He braked hard to make the right turn into the gas station driveway. He pulled abreast and to the left of the other Highway Patrol car and looked it over.

Dear God! Two uniformed officers were lying on the asphalt pavement. A man in a green sweatshirt aimed a pistol at their car and fired a shot, shattering the windshield.

Skip had the radio microphone in his hand in order to notify dispatch of their arrival. Instead, he screamed, "11-99, 11-99! SHOTS FIRED, J'S RES-TAURANT!"

He threw down the mike and dived out of the car. The man was still firing.

• • •

As the unit slid to a stop adjacent and just to the left of Walt and Roger's car, Mike saw the still form of Walt Frago before him. He felt on the seat beside him, located, and automatically put on his hat. He reached for the radio micro-phone but the dash hook was empty. Skip Pence had it and was screaming that they were 10-97, and 11-99, "shots fired." As he reached for the door handle, the familiarity of the scene flashed through Mike's mind. He had done this hundreds of times. Here they were arriving at the scene of an emergency. Be-fore him lay the battered and mutilated bodies to which they would administer first aid or unofficial last rites.

Everything would go smoothly now. They were here to bring calm to the chaos. The acrid odor of cordite would soon be replaced by the sulfur from the flares. The unworldly reddish hue created by the gas station's lights and unit 78-8's red spot would soon be diluted by the bright flashing lights of the ambu-lance and tow trucks. After making inquiry of the witnesses, taking pictures, and measurements for the official report, he and Skip would go to the hospital to interview the survivors. Golden State Hospital on Lyons Avenue, most likely, he reasoned. Most victims from Highway 99 mishaps were taken there.

He saw a man in a yellow jacket aiming a pistol. He flinched as this round also hit their windshield.

"Mike, look out!" he heard Skip shout. Mike had the shotgun in his hand

and leaped clear of the seat. Only then did he realize he was standing directly in the line of fire of the two men crouching behind the front of the Pontiac. Out of the corner of his eye, he saw Skip heading toward the rear of their unit. He ran instead to the back of Gore and Frago's car. He saw the man in the sweatshirt and another man climb into the Pontiac. He could hear shots. Skip! He moved down the right side of the 78-8 unit. He racked the slide on the pump. The noise was unmistakable. He saw one of the men raise his head from the driver's side of the Pontiac and fire a shot at him. At the same time, an unexpended round flew out of the side of the shotgun. Shit! He must have cocked it once before during his run from the patrol car. One of the men was in the back seat of the Pontiac. Mike fired. As if by magic, he saw a five-inch circular hole appear in the rear window of the car and the rest of the glass crystallize.

The man in the yellow jacket jumped out of the driver's door and began firing at Mike over the roof of the car. Mike returned fire. The shotgun was empty! Now the one in the yellow jacket ran around to the front of the Pontiac. Mike retreated to the rear of Unit 78-8, pulling out his revolver as he did so. He dropped the shotgun to the pavement and began to fire his revolver at the man over the left rear corner of the trunk. The man no longer was armed with a pistol; he now had a sawed-off shotgun. Where was he? Mike couldn't see him. He raised up over the trunk and tried to look through the rear window of the patrol car. Most of the glass in the car was shattered and spider-webbed. Mike still couldn't see him. He moved to his left and crouched behind the left rear fender. There he was, the guy in the yellow jacket was near the front of Unit 78-12, less than twenty feet away, pointing the sawed-off shotgun at him.

Mike raised his .357, but before he could squeeze off, the shotgun fired. All nine pellets of the .12 gauge double aught buckshot struck him in the face and upper torso. George Michael Alleyn fell forward onto the trunk of the vehicle and then collapsed to the ground. He was still alive. Somewhere in his subconscious roamed the thought that he would have to visit the hospital emergency room that night. Probably at the Golden State, as they were just off Highway 99. He thought of the nurse in the white stockings. He hated emergency rooms.

• • •

Skip ran to the rear of his unit, taking cover and drawing his revolver. He couldn't figure out what was happening, but he knew it was bad. Was that Roger lying there? And Walt? What in God's name had happened!

As the bullets began hitting the patrol car, all doubt as to the seriousness of the situation vanished.

There were two men—one in a yellow windbreaker, the other in a sweatshirt. Both were back in the Pontiac. He thought he heard Mike firing the shotgun.

Skip began shooting with his service revolver. Before realizing it was empty, he had clicked the trigger three times on spent chambers. He squatted behind the vehicle in order to load. Crouched as he was, the bullets wouldn't fall free of the cartridge pouch. He adjusted his position and the six rounds fell from the pouch into his hand pointing in different directions. As he fumbled, trying to get them aimed into the cylinder, he dropped two rounds. He finally got four loaded.

He felt a sharp pain in his left leg and knew he'd been shot. Because he wasn't standing, he couldn't tell if it was serious. Only the pain was apparent. He thought he felt his legs being hit again, and then again.

Before snapping shut the cylinder of his revolver, he looked on the ground for the cartridges he had dropped. He found one and picked it up. As he was placing it into the cylinder, he felt, more than heard, the presence of someone behind him.

"Now I've got you, you bastard!" the man screamed.

Skip rotated quickly to his left, looking up over his shoulder. Now, less than one foot away stood the man in the sweatshirt with a large automatic pistol.

They looked into each other's eyes.

Skip snapped shut the cylinder on his Smith and Wesson, but its click was drowned by the roar of the .45 automatic held by the other man.

James R. Pence Jr. didn't feel the damage inflicted by the 245-grain .45 caliber slug as it penetrated his skull just over the left eye.

FIFTY-ONE

In Unit 78-16R officers Ed Holmes and Richard Robinson overheard the radio traffic between 78-8 and Newhall dispatch and the subsequent car-to-car traffic between Gore and Frago to Pence and Alleyn. They were on Valencia Boulevard in the Saugus area less than three miles away.

Holmes was driving and made a U-turn through the parking lot of the Thatcher Glass Company when he heard that the stop was to be made at Valencia and Highway 99.

"Let's go give them a hand, Robbie," Holmes said.

The next transmission from Roger Gore said the red Pontiac was turning off early at Henry Mayo. Holmes speeded up. "Ain't that just like the public?" he said. "They never do what they're supposed to."

When the 11-99, officer needs help, was put out by Pence, Holmes pulled out all stops. Red light, siren. The big Dodge shot down the narrow road. As they rounded the right-hand curve onto the old highway, Holmes saw two patrol cars and a red Pontiac stopped in the service station driveway. He braked to a stop, and Robinson leaped out with the .12 gauge shotgun. Almost immediately, he drew up on a young man who was approaching with a revolver in his hand.

He yelled and the man stopped. He was shouting and pointing toward the patrol cars. Now Robinson could see a man in a yellow jacket running toward the Pontiac. Just before climbing in, the man fired a shot in their direction. Robinson thought he heard it strike the patrol car. He ran to a small fence dividing the parking lot from the road and poked the shotgun over it. The Pontiac was accelerating out of the station. He aimed at it but didn't squeeze the trigger. Because of the angle, the gas station and people in the building were in his line of fire. He heard another shot and saw the rear window of the Pontiac shatter. Ed Holmes had hit it with a shot from his revolver.

The Pontiac disappeared, and Robinson swung over the fence and approached the two patrol cars parked in the gas station lot. One had the windshield blown out.

"Oh, my God!" He saw one, then two, then three fallen bodies. All were in uniform, spots of red clearly visible on the tan fabric. The garish contrast between bloody smears and clean uniforms stunned him! Shocked and horrified, he approached the unmoving bodies.

He knelt and checked for signs of life. He was sick to his stomach as he recognized Roger Gore. And then Walt Frago. And Skip Pence.

Ed Holmes approached. "They went into a dead end!" he called. "Let's..." Then he saw the forms on the pavement.

"Just call it in! For God's sake, these three are dead!"

As Holmes ran for their car, Robinson walked back toward the patrol vehicles. He must be going into shock, he thought. He felt nothing. Only emptiness and disbelief. Those guys were Highway Patrolmen. They were dead. He heard the radio going crazy. Units from all over giving their locations and estimated response times. The sergeant being notified. Confirmation that the ambulances were rolling. He was numb.

Robinson leaned on the nearest patrol car for support. He was between the two bullet-riddled units now. He caught a flicker of movement out of the corner of his eye. Directly behind the other patrol car. He ran over. There was another officer lying there, but he was moving his arms and legs.

Thank God, he was alive! Robinson raced over and knelt beside him. He couldn't recognize the officer. His face and head were a mess of blood. Please God, please let him live! Maybe it's not too bad. Minor scalp and facial wounds bled profusely. Then he heard the weak, rasping breath. And he knew it was serious.

"Ed!" he shouted. "Get the first aid kit. He's alive." Holmes hurried over with the kit. By now, sirens wailed from several directions.

"See if you can do something," Robinson pleaded. "I'll try to see what happened to the guys who did this."

"Who is it?" asked Holmes, kneeling beside the now still form. Robinson ignored the question as he picked up his shotgun and started through the station lot.

• • •

Another unit arrived—78-19R with Officers Harry Ingold and Roger Palmer.

"Come on!" Robinson yelled to the two officers. "They're out this way." He gestured toward the station.

Robinson went around to the rear while the others went through the pump islands toward the road which bordered the station lot on the north.

Trucks were parked on the far side. The officers searched their undersides.

At one point, Ingold almost fired on a driver who moved suddenly inside the cab of a tanker.

There it was! Robinson stopped short. The Pontiac. Sitting at the dead end of the road which led east off old 99. The lights were on and the motor running. License number OSY 805. Already, it was more familiar to him than the license on his personal car. The vehicle was obviously abandoned, but he was still taking no chances.

He moved over to Ingold who had also spotted the vehicle. He was crouched at the front of a Kenworth which was hooked to a van type trailer with a reefer unit. The small refrigerator motor was running.

"Let's spread out and keep it covered till we're sure there's nobody in it," Robinson said. "Tell Palmer to cross the road and cover the driver's side. I can watch the front and right side from here. You get some place where you can shoot into the back if you have to."

Ingold moved off to give the word to Palmer.

Robinson stood and stretched his legs. The hell with it, he thought. Maybe I'll rush it. Chances are, whoever was in it has split. Before he could move, Sgt. Bill Walker was standing beside him. With him was Officer Toliver Miller, who had responded from Castaic Scale and still wore his tan coveralls. Officers Jack Burniston and Dave Dievendorf, operating Unit 78-15, also came up to the group.

"That's the car," said Robinson, pointing out the Pontiac. "Ingold and Palmer are over there."

"Okay, you guys cover us," Walker said to those with him. "Come on, Robbie, let's check it out."

With extreme caution, they approached the vehicle. As Robinson had guessed, it was empty.

"All right, come on!" Walker called indicating the vacant field to the north. "He must have gone down that way. Spread out and be careful!"

FIFTY-TWO

"Jesus, here come two more!" Bobby yelled. He and Jack ran for the car, "Get in!" he screamed. He jammed the key into the ignition. The engine roared to life.

Jack still held a revolver and was firing at the cruiser which had stopped out on the road.

"Go! Go!" Jack shrieked.

The cops returned fire. The back window blew out completely.

"God damn! Get the hell out!"

Leaving the engine running and the lights shining, Bobby grabbed a four-inch revolver from the floor of the car, shoved it into his belt, and picked up a two-inch revolver from the seat. In his other hand he clutched the .357 he'd taken from the cop. He jumped out and sprinted away from the car.

FIFTY-THREE

A shot rang out. David William Carpenter, a gas station attendant performing a lube job, ran to the rear of the lube room and hid behind a tool chest.

• • •

Twenty-four young people ranging in age from thirteen to twenty left the bus belonging to Del Aire Assembly of God Church Choir and charged into the diner for a midnight snack. Accompanying them were four adults. It had been an exhausting day. They had traveled from the Los Angeles area to Lamont, California, near Bakersfield, for a singing engagement and were on their way home.

The bus was parked in the lot.

One of the adults, Joe L. Ball, was thankful to have found J's open. Up the road, they had tried two other restaurants. One had been too full, and the other was closing. As he sat at one of the booths, he heard popping noises coming from out on the lot. Kids must be fooling with firecrackers, he thought. Seems like they get started earlier every year. He heard one of the choir members shout. "Hey! Those men are shooting the cops!"

He ran to the window as a second Highway Patrol car roared into the lot. He couldn't believe what was happening! Guns going off and people getting shot and falling dead.

"Mary Owens is still on the bus!" someone yelled. "She was asleep and nobody woke her up."

Ball raced from the diner and out to the bus. On the way, he saw still another CHP car pull up. Officers fired at the back of a red Pontiac. He reached the bus and ran to the back seat. Mary Owens was stretched out flat, not moving. Oh, dear Lord, had she been hit by a stray bullet? No, she was only sleeping.

• • •

Matthew Barth was exhausted. He'd been up most of the previous night working as manager of the Bucket, a nude dance bar in Hawthorne. Early that morning, he and his friend Joe Tancredi had taken his boat and two of the girls from the show up to Lake Ming near Bakersfield.

After they had stopped at J's, Tancredi, who had been following Barth, mentioned that the boat trailer lights were flickering. The two men had left the restaurant to try to determine the cause. Their attention had been diverted slightly by the arrival of the red Pontiac and Unit 78-8.

"Somebody's getting busted," Tancredi remarked.

When the first shots rang out, Barth couldn't believe his eyes. He figured it had to be some kind of training exercise. Once he saw the first officer fall, he knew it was real.

"Jesus Christ, Joe!" he shouted. "Look out that you don't get hit."

The warning was unnecessary. Joe Tancredi had already run up to position himself between the boat and the pickup. He was crouching behind a rear fender of the truck. Matt Barth joined him.

"What the hell's going on?" Joe said.

"Don't know. But you'd better check on Karen. She's sleeping in the front," Barth said.

Tancredi crept along the left side of the pickup. He found his girlfriend crouched on the floorboards inside the cab. "Stay down, honey!" he shouted.

By now, the second unit had arrived and once again the two men watched.

"Oh, Lord. The goddamned bad guys are winning," Joe said. They watched as a civilian ran out and picked up a shotgun. Then he picked up one of the officer's pistols and began shooting. At almost the same time, a third CHP car arrived. The two men jumped into the Pontiac. They drove through the station and out of sight.

"I don't believe it!" Tancredi said once the shooting had stopped.

"Me neither," Barth said, "but it sure as hell happened. Right there in front of us."

• • •

Janice Carol Bible was upset. She'd been called in for extra duty. It was like she had an obligation or something. After all, she was just the hired help—a hash slinger. She'd put in her shift already today—6 a.m. to 2 p.m.

As she parked her pickup, she noted the bus in the center of the parking lot. "Del Aire Assembly of God." There were several other cars, one with a nice looking boat. Oh well, she sighed. Al Sims was a good boss. She glanced inside. From the look of things he needed help. The place was a madhouse. Thirty or forty high-school age kids filling the booths and lining the counter. Other people crowded around the cash register. She'd never seen so many customers at one time.

She was walking along the northern end of the restaurant when she heard someone shout, "Get your hands up and keep them up!" Instinctively, she began to raise her hands as she turned to her right, the direction of the sound. She felt slightly foolish as she realized that it was a police officer standing beside a red car over in the gas station driveway, at least fifty feet distant. As she turned the corner and neared the front door, she heard the voice once more. "We told you to get your hands up!"

Probably another dope bust, she thought as she opened the door to the building and was greeted by the bedlam within.

• • •

Gary Dean Kness was on his way to work. He liked the night shift at Hydraulic Research Corporation. As he made a right turn onto the Old Highway off Henry Mayo Drive, he saw two Highway Patrol cars stopped behind a red Pontiac in the Standard station. He became aware of a strange popping sound. Then he could see the officers, one behind each car. He saw flashes. My God, they're shooting at someone, he thought. He pulled his white Thunderbird to the right and stopped. He could see one of the officers. He had a shotgun in his hands, pointing it over the roof of the patrol car at the Pontiac. He's been hit! The officer was now slumped on the rear fender of the unit. Then the officer crumpled forward, falling out from behind the car.

In a moment, Kness was out of his car and running toward the officer. He had to help him, get him out of the line of fire. Approaching the fallen man, Kness could see he was young and his face was covered with blood. He bent over and grabbed the gun belt and tried to pull the officer back in behind the car. He glanced up to see a man approaching with what looked like a sawed-off shotgun in his hand. Again, without thinking, Kness picked up the shotgun the officer had held. As he aimed at the advancing man, he could see still another uniformed officer lying on the ground to the front of the cruiser. He vaguely heard shots from behind the other patrol car. Click! The gun was empty!

He tried to pump it. It clicked again. Frantic now, he reached down and picked up a revolver lying next to the officer's hand. The wooden grip was sticky and warm with blood. The man was even closer, creeping along the left side of the patrol car. With both hands, Kness raised the revolver. Pointing it in the direction of the man, he jerked the trigger. He was startled and partially blinded by the unexpected explosion as the magnum round fired. The man was turning and starting to run. Kness took aim at the retreating back and pulled the trigger. Nothing happened. He pulled the trigger again but the hammer fell on an empty chamber.

He could hear more shots and shouting to his left. He saw another officer collapse grotesquely. Panic overtook him. He ran back toward his car. Still another Highway Patrol car was coming. An officer jumped out of the right side and pointed a shotgun at him. Kness didn't fully realize it, but he was very close to dying.

"Wait, there's two guys up there with guns! Three officers shot!" The shotgun didn't lower—then he realized that he was still clutching the revolver.

"There!" he gasped. He pointed and the two men rushed toward the Pontiac.

An officer jumped from behind the wheel of the patrol car that had just arrived. He fired a shot at the pair as they fled. One stopped and returned fire. Kness could hear the impact as it struck the cruiser. Both officers dived for cover.

Using vehicles and shrubbery for cover, the two officers from the third patrol car hurried forward.

Gary Dean Kness walked over to his car and sat down. He let the revolver slip to the floor. He was going to be sick.

FIFTY-FOUR

Bobby could hear Jack yelling for him to come back and take more weapons and money.

To hell with it! Get away! That was the main thing. He raced ahead leaving the bright lights of the station behind. He ran in total darkness and immediately fell down a sloping bank. He was too scared and too frantic to tell if he were hurt. If he were, he didn't feel it.

On his feet again, he ran parallel to the freeway on his right. Ahead, dimly visible, he saw what looked like a light-colored wall. As he ran closer to it, he saw that it was a bank of white boulders, probably for erosion control. He figured that on the other side would be water. As he tried to scale the bank, he slipped on the dew-covered rocks. He kept his balance but dropped the two-inch revolver. He fumbled to find it, but the ground was pitch black.

He raced on up over the boulders, crawling and running. Now he could see stars reflecting from the water. He held his breath and jumped. His feet sliced through the surface and struck the graveled bottom. The jolt caused his knees to buckle. His teeth clamped together and he almost fell. This time he dropped the pistol in his hand, but he could still see it in the six-inch deep water. It was cold as he bent to retrieve it. He splashed across the stream and turned to his right. This took him under the freeway bridge.

"This way!" he shouted, listening carefully to see if he could locate Jack by ear. Noise from the vehicles passing overhead drowned out everything else. Maybe Jack would slip them and they could both get back to the apartment.

As he came out from under the highway overcrossing, he could see nothing but dark hills ahead. He heard what sounded like dozens of sirens. They spurred him to a steady trot directly away from the highway.

As long as there was darkness in front of him and there was increasing distance behind, he knew he could make it. Besides, he could see better now. Away from the highway and the strong neons of the businesses, the stars, without competition, softly lighted the landscape.

He spotted what appeared to be a trail leading off to the northeast. He followed it, alternating between a trot and a walk. As far as he could tell, there was no human life around him. The road he was following, little more than worn tire tracks in the wild oats, began a gentle climb. Soon he saw lights to the east. A town, but a small one. Probably several miles away. He kept on going.

The night was quiet, the sound of the sirens fading to nothing. He stopped to rest and check the guns. The cop's gun was empty. He almost chucked it then and there. Better not, he reasoned. Guns always seemed to come in handy. The four-inch .357 in his belt held only one live round. He cursed as he threw the five expended cartridge cases into the darkness. Carefully, he turned the cylinder so that the round would rotate into firing position when the trigger was pulled.

He set off walking instead of running. Might as well save what energy he had left. The terrain was getting steeper. The excitement, the fear and the run had given him an incredible thirst. He wondered if he were going out into the desert. The Mojave was somewhere near, he knew. The very thought increased his thirst. He considered bearing off to his right to see if he would hit the creek again. No, that would take him in the direction of the lights, toward the town. He was better off in the boondocks. He needed water, not civilization.

He stopped short, holding his breath for fear it would give him away. Twenty to thirty yards in front of him was a dark form. Something on it had caused a glint. A car perhaps? Yes, there was a car parked in the path. He tiptoed toward it. A pickup with a camper attached. He moved slowly forward, loaded gun at the ready. He strained to listen for any sounds but heard nothing.

He saw that the truck was an older model, an International Scout with a homemade box on the back. Sneaking up to it, he gingerly tried one front door and then the other. Locked. He circled to the back. His feet crunched in the pea gravel so he tried walking on the outside edges of his soles. He turned the knob on the rear door. It too was locked.

Strapped above the rear bumper was a five-gallon G.I. can. Bobby hoped against hope that it contained water. He tapped the lid of the can with the heel of his hand. It gave easily enough, but when he began to unscrew it, it squeaked.

He heard a rustle inside the truck. Quickly, he squatted. A flashlight shined out the back and side windows. He waited, silent, hardly daring to breathe. The flashlight went off. He felt the truck sway slightly as whoever it was lay back down.

He knew that soon it was going to be dawn. He had to get clear of the area or find a way of hiding out. Staying here on foot was probably best, he thought, but he knew he couldn't make it without water. Then again, it would be better if he could somehow steal the truck and drive while it was dark. Once outside the immediate area, he'd abandon the truck and steal a car. No matter what, Bobby knew he had to do something, not just squat there all night.

He stood and crept around the side of the truck. In the wooden sides were louvered, ventilation windows. He hammered the butt of the four-inch pistol against a glass panel. It shattered.

"What the hell's going on?" a male voice called from inside.

"Get out of there!" Bobby yelled.

"No. Go away!"

"I said, get *out*!" He thumped the side of the camper with the pistol.

"What do you want?"

Did the voice sound pleading? Scared? "I want your truck! Now, now get the hell out."

"I've got a gun!"

"I've got one too, you son-of-a-bitch! Get out of that truck!"

The tip of a gun barrel suddenly stuck out the broken window. A shot rang out. Even though the bullet was fired away from where Bobby stood, the flash momentarily blinded him. There were two more shots.

God damn! Bobby was amazed. This made the second time that night that some square john had shot at him!

He reached up and fired the .357 into the camper. "Now we're even, you stupid bastard!"

Silence. Had he hit him? He had no way of knowing. Everything was still.

"Listen," he shouted, "either you come out, or I'm going to shoot your gas tank and burn up your ass. Hear me?"

"All right, I'll come out."

"Throw your gun out first."

"No. I'm going to keep my gun."

"Throw it out or I'll kill you the minute I see you."

"No," the man insisted, "I'm going to keep my gun! I have to put on some clothes."

Bobby crept around to the left side of the camper and hid. He took the empty six-inch revolver from his belt and held it by the barrel. As soon as the man emerged through the door, he swung as hard as he could at his head.

The blow was a glancing one. The man screamed and ran down the trail. Bobby gave chase. He couldn't let him get away. Without warning, the man whirled and began firing a pistol.

Bobby hit the dirt and began to roll. Then he was up and leaped for the man. He was stunned by the explosion of the pistol and felt a tremendous impact to his neck and right shoulder. His momentum carried him into the man and they fell. Bobby swung the pistol savagely at the man's head. Several swings later, the man lay still.

Pain and nausea caught up with Bobby. He realized he'd been shot. It felt like his collar bone. There was blood running down his chest and stomach. He stumbled to the camper. His thirst was overpowering. He looked for a first aid kit or something to stop the bleeding. The truck was so cluttered he couldn't find anything resembling a bandage. He located a plastic water jug and drank it dry. He ripped off his t-shirt and pressed it against the wound. He felt dizzy.

Ironic. He had made it through a hell of a gun battle with four, no six, cops shooting at him and had only gotten cut by some glass. Now some old man out here in the sticks shoots him and damned near does him in. He couldn't walk and hide out on foot with the wound. He was already feeling weak. Loss of blood? Shock? Maybe both.

He left the camper and walked back to the man who lay where he'd fallen. The bastard was still conscious and moaning. Kneeling next to him, Bobby gave him a halfhearted swipe on the side of his head with the revolver. "Where are the keys to the truck?"

"Inside. They're inside," came the muffled response.

Bobby swung again at the back of the head twice, with all the force he could muster. He returned to the camper and leaned into the cab. The keys were in the ignition. He reached through and unlocked the driver's door. With just a glance in the direction of the truck's owner, he pulled himself behind the wheel, started the engine, and drove down the path. Soon he came to a paved road. He turned left, once again heading away from the general direction of the shooting.

PART THREE
AFTERMATH

FIFTY-FIVE

Daniel Joseph Schwartz lay still on the ground. He turned his head slowly to watch his International Scout disappear into the darkness. He knew he was hurt and wondered how badly. Thoughts of concussion and paralysis accompanied the throbbing pain in his head. He tried to move his arms, then his legs. He sat up. The pain became unbearable, but quickly receded. Got to move more slowly, he thought, as he got his feet under him. Slowly, painfully, he stood and moved his head from side to side to clear it.

What had happened? Where had that crazy guy come from? In his forty years of life, he had never seen anything like it. The guy had tried to kill him. He had stolen his truck and all his possessions. What he'd heard about California must be true. The place was full of lunatics.

Now what should he do? Tell the police. He recalled passing some kind of power station just where he turned off the main road. About a mile, he estimated. Could he make it? He took a timid step. All right. His strength and balance were returning.

Funny, he wasn't too sore. He felt his head. Lumps and cuts on his head, but not a lot of blood. He wasn't sure if he'd lost consciousness in the struggle, but he'd sure caught a couple on the noggin. Everybody had always called him a hard head, he thought. He supposed they were right.

As soon as he could, he was going to get out of here. Get away from the West Coast and back to the Midwest where people were more down to earth. Maybe head south. The folks were friendlier there too. Never, in all his travels, had he had an experience like this. He had left his home in Chicago nearly two years ago now. Put all his belongings in the Scout and had just driven off. Kind of a modern day gypsy. Traveling around, working if he felt like it, moving on when he didn't. The folks in Chicago couldn't understand it. A grown man running around the country like a vagabond. They'd tried to dissuade him, but he went anyhow. He *could* be hardheaded when he wanted to be. But this was it. He had to leave California.

He walked as best he could along the trail and back to the road. He saw a sign on the chain link gate. It was barely readable in the starlight. "San Francisco/Green Valley Maintenance Yard #2, Private Property, Pacific Gas and Electric Company." The place looked deserted. Inside was a tin building that looked like a Quonset hut. Maybe there was somebody there, somebody who could help. He yelled and shook the gate, which caused a blinding pain in his head. A light came on in the building.

Within a few minutes, he was inside and talking to the Sheriff's Department on the telephone. "I was parked on a dirt road by the power station on..." He looked inquiringly at the crewman.

"Station #2 on San Francisquito Road," the man said. Schwartz relayed the information, stumbling on the unfamiliar Spanish name. As rapidly as he was able, he related the story to the deputy. He gave a complete description of his vehicle but was unable to say much about his assailant.

"Stay right there. We'll send an ambulance," the deputy instructed as he turned to notify Sheriff's dispatch.

FIFTY-SIX

Immediately after receiving the emergency 11-99 call from Skip Pence in Unit 78-12, Dispatcher Jo Ann Tidey repeated it to all units and all stations. When she received the word from Officer Holmes that three officers had been shot, she immediately called the ambulance from the Golden State Hospital and notified the Los Angeles Sheriff's Department in the event they had not monitored the broadcast. Next she notified the other shift supervisor, Sgt. Paul Connel. He directed that she notify 78-C, Capt. Bob Goode, the Area Commander. Capt. Goode in turn requested that she advise L. A. dispatch to notify supervising Inspector George Reinjohn, the Zone Commander. He notified CHP headquarters in Sacramento, requesting that Commissioner Harold Sullivan be contacted.

• • •

Once the three officers' deaths were confirmed, the Newhall Sheriff's sub-station called L. A. Sheriff homicide investigator Sgt. John Brady and the L. A. County Coroner's Office.

• • •

Under the direction of Sgts. Connel and Walker, roadblocks were set up at strategic locations throughout northern Los Angeles County. The only information given out was the meager description obtained from diners at J's Restaurant and from Gary Dean Kness. "Two men, average size, possibly in their late twenties. One was wearing a dark green pullover sweatshirt-type parka; the other a yellow jacket." They were on foot, armed, and should be considered dangerous.

• • •

Sgt. George Griffith, working in the Ventura Area, sent his only graveyard unit to set up a roadblock at the Los Angeles/Ventura County line on Highway 126, approximately twenty miles to the west.

• • •

CHP officer George Michael Alleyn died en route to Golden State Hospital.

• • •

Capt. Goode arrived and ordered that a command post be established at the Castaic Scale facility less than a mile away.

• • •

Sgt. Brady, Los Angeles Sheriff's Office investigator, arrived and put his identification unit to work photographing and gathering evidence at the crime scene. There was a preliminary search of the Pontiac, and a temporary registration was found with the name Russell Lowell Talbert, III.

• • •

Capt. Goode and Lt. Court West, second in command of the Newhall Area, went to notify the four young wives that they were widows.

• • •

At thirty minutes past midnight, Dr. C. Hegeman, night resident at the Golden State Hospital, officially pronounced Roger David Gore, Walter Carroll Frago, James Edward Pence, Jr., and George Michael Alleyn dead.

• • •

Capt. Louis Brown, Commander of Lancaster Area, immediately to the east, ordered his units to set up roadblocks on Highways 14 and 138. He then responded to Newhall and took charge of the command post at the Castaic Truck Scale.

• • •

At 0152, a drunk driver ran off the road and struck a utility pole on Highway 138, two miles east of Interstate 5. Although in Newhall Area's jurisdiction, it was requested that it be investigated by a unit from the adjoining Lancaster Area.

• • •

0200 Hours. Newhall dispatch issued this broadcast:

"Newhall to all units and stations. BOLO, two suspects on foot. Last seen in the area of Highway 99 and Henry Mayo Drive.

"Suspect number one is described as a white male adult, late 20's, approximately 5 foot 9, 160, wearing a yellow zipper jacket.

"Suspect number two, a white male adult, approximately 30-35 years, 6 foot, 160, wearing a green sweatshirt with a hood. No further descriptions.

"These subjects were involved in a 187 P.C. of four CHP officers in the

Newhall Area at 2355 past date. Any information this station, Newhall clear: KMV 386."

· · ·

0202 hours. Officers Lloyd Bridge and Jack Upton, working in the West Los Angeles Area, heard the scant details of the shooting put out on the all-points bulletin and positioned their unit at Mulholland Drive where they could watch traffic southbound on the San Diego freeway. Twenty to thirty minutes later, they observed a vehicle go by at more than a hundred miles per hour. They pursued it and made the stop at Wilshire Boulevard. Their adrenaline escalated when they observed several spent rifle cartridges on the floorboard. The driver's explanation was that he and his buddy had been out shooting in the Newhall-Saugus area. A .41 caliber magnum pistol and .30 caliber carbine were discovered hidden under the front seat. Both of the occupants were arrested and booked for suspicion of murder. Once it was determined that they had not been involved, the charge was reduced to carrying a concealed weapon.

· · ·

At 0240 hours, a property damage accident occurred at the intersection of Interstate 5 and Highway 14. Again, a Lancaster unit handled it.

· · ·

At 0317 hours, Commissioner Harold Sullivan arrived at the Castaic Scale facility via CHP helicopter. A former Los Angeles Police Department Assistant Chief, he had come to offer his assistance and the knowledge accumulated in more than three decades of being a policeman.

· · ·

By 0330, an extensive ground search had been conducted with the aid of CHP and Sheriff's helicopters. Although the entire freeway and surrounding roadway system was under surveillance, no suspects had been located.

· · ·

As all these events transpired, Jo Ann Tidey performed almost mechanically. Upon hearing the initial call for help from Unit 78-12, she slipped into the routine she had been trained for. Her radio transmissions remained unemotional, the required notifications automatically carried out. When she received orders from the responding supervisors, she dutifully repeated them to the other units.

Yet, she was out there with them. Connected only by the radio waves, she was an integral part of everything that was happening.

She heard the sound of the sirens rushing by on Highway 99. As the graveyard shift arrived, Jo Ann Tidey was led to the office lounge where she collapsed, weeping uncontrollably.

FIFTY-SEVEN

0415 Hours: Los Angeles County Sheriff's Deputies Fred Thatcher and Don Yates, assigned to the Antelope Valley Substation, received a radio call to be on the lookout for a green 1963 International Scout pickup with a home-made camper, Illinois license number 553376. There was a possibility that the driver was involved in the shooting of the four CHP officers.

San Francisquito Canyon Road was to be sealed off on both the Saugus and Lancaster ends. Heading west from Lancaster, the deputies pulled onto San Francisquito and, using their car, set up a roadblock. Within minutes, they saw lights approaching.

• • •

Bobby couldn't figure it out. What was happening? He knew he'd been driving in kind of a daze, not paying much attention, but what were the lights ahead? There shouldn't be lights way out here. He felt tired. The bullet wound, the strain, he didn't know which, had made him weak. He was driving slowly, afraid to push the old wreck much faster. He came within fifty feet of the Sheriff's unit before he recognized it as a police car. Then it was too late. He pulled to a halt.

He could see officers now. The same tan uniforms the Highway Patrol had worn. One of them yelled for him to get out, his hands in sight. The deputy carried a sawed-off shotgun.

Bobby had a gun, the old English Enfield pistol he'd taken from the truck's owner, but it was empty. Shit! Should he try and run for it? Not in this ancient rattletrap. On foot? It was still dark, but not for long. Both of the cops had guns trained on him. Try to take them? No chance. They would kill him for sure. But might that be better than being caught and going back to prison?

"You heard me. Step out of there with your hands up!" It was the one pointing the shotgun over the rear of the car.

Bobby climbed out slowly, leaving the empty Enfield on the seat of the truck. He lay face down in the road with his arms spread. Jesus Christ, he was cold. He wondered if he were going into shock. Could a person tell when his body temperature was getting dangerously low? Was his blood pressure weakening and his pulse slowing? He would welcome the unconsciousness that was supposed to follow.

• • •

The Sheriff's deputies were being extremely cautious. They suspected that there was another person in the truck. They had radioed for a second unit to back them up before they left their positions of advantage and approached the vehicle.

"Hey, goddammit," Bobby complained, "I'm freezing to death! And I'm wounded. I need to see a doctor!"

"Shut up and don't move."

Bobby's body began to shake, racked by spasms of chill and pain. He sobbed involuntarily. "Help me. Please help me," he moaned.

Within ten minutes, another L. A. County Sheriff's car arrived with two more deputies. They held a brief conference, then deployed in the darkness surrounding the Scout.

• • •

One stepped up to Bobby and put a pistol to his head. "Move and it will be all over," the deputy threatened. Bobby could feel the muzzle pushing into the base of his skull. He tried to stop shivering. He lay still while they roughly frisked him. His hands were forced behind him and cuffs placed on his wrists.

"Get up!"

"I...I can't." He was nudged in the ribs by a boot toe. The command was repeated. Bobby tried to move his feet up under him. He couldn't make them respond. The toe nudged again. Another Sheriff car arrived. It was a sergeant. "The truck's empty," someone said. "We've got one though!"

"Get him into the car, I want to talk to him," came the harsh reply.

Bobby felt himself being lifted, half-dragged and half-carried. He was placed in the rear of a patrol car. The sergeant sat beside him. Bobby looked at the unsympathetic face. "Man, I've been hurt," he said, teeth chattering. "I need to go to a doctor."

There was no response.

"Let's go," the sergeant said. "Golden State!"

Bobby leaned back and tried to gather his thoughts. The sergeant was quoting the Miranda, warning about his right to an attorney, to remain silent, and the alternatives. Bobby knew that they could probably tie him into the Pontiac through fingerprints. Also, they had him cold on the stolen truck. He couldn't explain that away, nor the gunshot wound in his chest. The handcuffs were pinching his wrists and the pressure of his body against his pinioned arms was causing numbness in his fingers.

"What's your name?" the sergeant asked. He held the contents of Bobby's wallet in his hand, examining the cards and identification.

"Russell Lowell Talbert."

The sergeant checked the North Carolina driver's license and the California temporary license. "Want to tell me how you got hurt and what you were doing in that pickup truck?"

"Well, earlier today, I was hitchhiking and a couple of guys picked me up. They were some bad cats. We were on Highway 99, I think, when they got stopped by the cops and everybody started shooting. I ran. Tried to get the hell out of there. I ran up in the hills and came across the truck parked there. There was a guy in it. When I asked him to let me in, he shot me. Then he came out and I hit him and took the truck! I was scared!"

"Do you know who the guys were in the car that gave you the ride?"

"No."

"How many were there in the car?"

"Two. Three with me."

"Where did the shooting take place?"

"Hell, I don't know. It was a gas station or something right on the highway. Am I going to see a doctor?"

"Yeah, we're there now," said the sergeant, furiously scribbling notes in the black notebook he held.

Bobby was led into the rear emergency door of the Golden State Hospital and told to be seated on a gurney.

The sergeant removed the handcuffs and warned him not to try anything. Bobby wasn't in the frame of mind to try anything. He lay back and glanced across the room. There, lying similarly on a hospital litter, was a plump, balding, middle-aged man. His balding pate was laced with cuts and contusions, several displaying recently applied sutures.

From their respective reclining positions, neither recognized the other as his adversary of a couple hours earlier.

FIFTY-EIGHT

Jack stumbled and fell. In his left hand, he held a pistol—one of the officers'. In his right, he had the CHP pump shotgun. Under one arm was clamped
his own sawed-off shotgun.

"Bobby!" he whispered hoarsely. Where the hell was Bobby? Jesus Christ!
"Got to get the hell out of here," he muttered as he looked around. Nobody
following. What had happened to Bobby?

Sirens and lights—the whole world seemed full of them. Who'd have thought
there were so goddamned many cops out here in the sticks? No sense carrying
the sawed-off; he'd brought it for Bobby. He threw it down.

He ran west, in a near-blind panic, away from the lights and commotion.
He stumbled through a ditch and crossed a paved road. Nothing but darkness in
front of him.

He ran until he could go no further. The screaming of the sirens was well
behind him. He could hardly hear them above the rasp of his own breathing. He
stopped on top a rise and lay down. He turned to look back the way he'd come.
Still no pursuit. He got up and moved several yards to his left. He could see the
lights of the Standard station and the neon of J's Restaurant sign maybe a half
mile away. Occasionally, he saw the flashing lights of a police car entering or
leaving the freeway. As long as they stayed in their cars, they wouldn't get him,
he thought. As far as he could tell, there were no nearby roads. Back home,
they'd get dogs on his trail. He wondered if they used dogs here.

Man, was he ever in trouble! Big fuckin' trouble. But there'd been no choice.
The cops had gotten them cold. And where in the hell was Bobby? Had they
gotten him? Not without a fight. That little shit wouldn't go easy, Jack thought,
and he'd heard no more shooting. That meant he'd probably made it. But where?

Along with his returning breath came more rational thoughts. He had to
get some wheels. Get out of the sticks. Down to L. A. and get lost in the crowd.
He tried to reconstruct his flight and orient himself. He could see that the freeway was running left and right in front of him. Since the cafe and gas station
were on this side, and he and Bobby hadn't crossed over the highway to get to
them, L. A. must be to his right.

He got to his feet, for the first time noticing the guns in his hands. He placed the butt of the shotgun on the ground, leaning the barrel against his leg. He checked the revolver, a Colt with a six-inch barrel. He could make out the lettering in the moonlight, ".357 magnum Python." It had two expended shells and four live rounds in the cylinder. He pulled two bullets from his pants pocket and fully loaded the pistol. He slid it into his waistband. It didn't feel as solid as the .45 automatic had.

He became aware of a dull ache in his head and a distant ringing in his ears. He ran a hand across his forehead and felt a bump and a sharp pain. Another above his right eye. The blood was sticky, just beginning to congeal. It came back to him—the rear window of the car exploding and the searing burn on his forehead. He'd been shot. Nothing serious. The bleeding was almost stopped. It would take a hell of a lot more than that to get Jack Twining!

They'd not get him! No way was he going back inside. Besides, if all those cops were dead, they'd just put him in long enough to be hung.

He turned his attention to the shotgun. How the hell did it work? He located the slide release near the front of the trigger guard and pulled it. A live shell ejected onto the ground. He picked it up and pushed it into the feed on the bottom of the gun. He thrust his finger after it. Only slight movement. That meant it was fully loaded; four or five shells, he wasn't sure. He felt in his jacket pocket, another five or six shotgun shells there.

The moon and stars provided sufficient light for him to keep his direction reasonably constant. But the going was rough, and he couldn't see well enough to avoid rocks and holes. Until now, the terrain had been fairly smooth, but the hills were becoming steeper and the ground was covered with some kind of stickers that went right through his socks and tortured his ankles. A few scrub oaks were scattered on the hillsides, and clumps of mesquite and buck brush provided other obstacles.

Jack tried to keep the freeway in view to his left. To do so, he had to detour around steep ravines and banks. At one point, he walked into a barbed-wire fence. The impact frightened him and caused him to drop the shotgun. After climbing the fence, he went around a side hill until he could again view the highway. He could no longer see the gas station or restaurant, just a soft red glow.

He sat down, his back against one of the oaks. He was closer to the highway than he'd been before. He could see what he imagined to be a patrol car slowly heading north. It had an amber light flashing on its rear and a white spotlight playing on the hills on the far side of the freeway. Maybe that was a good sign. Maybe they didn't know which way he had gone.

He looked at the Bulova on his wrist. Still working. Ten minutes till two. What time had all this happened? Around midnight, he guessed. Maybe earlier. It seemed he'd been running for hours. He'd better keep going, see if he couldn't get somewhere before dawn. With daylight, he'd be easier to spot. They might use airplanes, or dogs.

He stepped up his pace. But now the moonlight was fading; he had to slow or continually stumble. At the bottom of one hill, he saw a large oblong gleaming object in his path, an old bathtub, filled with water An animal trough. He fell to his knees and drank, hardly tasting the liquid. Finally sated, he tried to wash his face, to get some of the blood off.

Jesus Christ, what's that? There was a dull wop-wop-wop and a droning noise overhead. He listened intently. A helicopter! They've got a friggin' helicopter! He crouched under a tree until the noise faded in the distance. Now he was certain he had to do something before the sun came up. He had seen enough episodes of "The FBI" on television to know the effectiveness of helicopters in finding fugitives. The numerous successes of Inspector Erskine attested to that.

Again he tried to go faster. Oh, shit! A paved road; he had almost walked out onto it. He crept back into the brush and listened. Nothing. He couldn't see the highway from his location but thought it must be close because he could hear the trucks and an occasional whine of tires.

He could tell from the horizon facing him that the ground on the far side of the pavement rose sharply. Rather than climb it, he followed the road to his left, toward the highway instead.

As he followed it around a sharp bend, he was startled by the abrupt appearance of civilization. Within two hundred yards on his side of the little road was a gas station, a bright yellow Shell sign at least forty feet off the ground. A little farther, a neon proclaimed, "Denny's, Open 24 Hours."

Maybe he could get a car at that station. The sight of white doors on the car turning around in the station driveway quickly dissuaded him. Better stay away, stick to the hills like he'd been doing. Cross the road here and just stay in the hills, following the freeway down. He had been right, the slope on the far side of the road was extremely steep. He was forced to stop and rest about halfway up. Now, off to his left, he had a good view of the highway. Beyond was a town. It looked pretty big to Jack. He tried to remember what towns they had driven through on this side of L. A.—Burbank, or Glendale? He didn't think so. There were cities and towns on both sides of the freeway there.

As Jack climbed the hill, he was alarmed by the barking of a dog. It seemed to be in front of him, a little to his right. He altered his course to the left and was shocked to discover a house right in front of him. A sprawling ranch style house on the crest of the hill. He was approaching its side or back, and there were lights on somewhere inside.

• • •

"Steve, honey, will you go out and see what's wrong with Tillie?" Betty Jean Hoag said. "She's been barking for the last fifteen minutes."

"All right." Steven Hoag put down his cup. "It's probably coyotes again. They've been coming in pretty close to try to get at the garbage."

It was shortly after 4 a.m. The Hoags were up early, but no earlier than usual. Hoag was a cement-truck driver for a local construction company, and, with all the building going on in the area, early starts and long days were the rule.

As he stepped out of the door and started around the corner of the house, a man with a shotgun suddenly loomed before him. A savage-looking man.

"Hold it right there!" he snarled pointing the gun directly at Hoag's chest.

The man's face was caked with blood, his eyes and hair wild, foxtails and star thistle clinging to his clothing.

"Listen you bastard, I'm not afraid to use this!" he snapped. "I need a car and a drink."

Hoag, dumbfounded, stared at the cold steel barrel.

"What's that back there?" the man asked indicating a room adjacent to the garage.

"M-my son sleeps there. He's seventeen. Please—"

"Shut up! Who else is in the house?"

"My wife," Hoag answered.

• • •

Betty Jean finished setting the table. She walked to the front of the house to call Steve in for breakfast. Through the still-opened front door, she saw a stranger pointing a gun. She ran to the phone and called the Highway Patrol. Because she had formerly been a stenographer for the Los Angeles Police Department, she knew that the proper authority to call was the Sheriff's Office, but she also knew that the Newhall CHP office was less than half a block away, at the bottom of the hill next to Denny's.

• • •

At 0430 hours Dispatcher Jo Ann Tidey received the call from Betty Jean Hoag that there was a man holding a gun on her husband. She gave her address as 27248 Pico Canyon Road, Newhall. Tidey immediately broadcast the information to all CHP units and relayed it to the Los Angeles Sheriff's Office.

• • •

"Inside!" Jack motioned for Hoag to go ahead of him. As they entered, Hoag told his wife, "This man wants to talk to us."

"Listen, I won't hurt you if you do what I say," the man told them. "I need some water. I don't want to shoot you, but I will if I have to. I've already shot three or four others tonight."

Betty Jean led the way into the kitchen. She was uncertain whether she had acted correctly in calling the police. She worried that any minute they might come roaring up to the house, and it was hard to tell what this crazy man would do. Should she tell her husband? Perhaps warn the man so he wouldn't be surprised and do something rash? Maybe try to convince him of the futility? If she told him that the Highway Patrol was coming and that they would be there any minute, would he panic? Kill them both? She looked helplessly at her husband and said nothing.

The man, seeing that breakfast was ready, sat down at the table and began to eat. The Hoags stood silently watching.

There was a slight tap at the front door.

"Is that your son?" the man snapped, starting to rise.

"Probably," Betty Jean said. "I'll get it." She went down the hall and opened the door to a uniformed sheriff's deputy.

"He's in the kitchen with my husband. He's got guns!" she whispered frantically. The deputy pulled her from the house and closed the door behind them.

• • •

Jack jumped to his feet and forced Hoag down the hall in front of him. Realizing now that he had permitted one hostage to escape, he rushed to the window. There in the drive was a Highway Patrol car. Mrs. Hoag and a youth, probably the son, were slipping behind it.

"Son-of-a-bitch!" he snarled. "Get your ass back in the kitchen! Shit! I wish to hell she hadn't done that!"

"Remember, you, out there," Jack shouted through the door, "I got this guy here and I got a gun!" Motioning Hoag to stay put, he opened the rear door and peered out. At the same instant, a sheriff's deputy came around the corner. Jack fired a quick round with the shotgun. Missed. He retreated back into the house.

"Where's that go?" he asked, pointing to the hallway running off the kitchen.

"To the bedrooms."

"Any doors back there?"

"No," replied Hoag.

"Okay then, we'll stay here in the kitchen. No windows, and I can watch the doors. Sit down and relax."

. . .

Hoag sat down, but he certainly couldn't relax. He was thankful and relieved that his family had reached safety but had no idea what would happen next. The man seemed to be calming down. That was good. "My name's Steve," he began with what he hoped would pass for a friendly smile.

"Shut up!"

Well, whatever was going to happen, the man with the gun seemed to be holding all the cards.

"Uh, my name's Jack," the man said, almost apologetically. In a noticeable drawl, he went on, "I don't want to hurt you. You know that, don't you?"

Hoag nodded.

"But I've got to try and figure a way out, and right now you're about the only hope I've got."

"You can count on me not to give you trouble. I don't want to see anybody get hurt either." He began to calm a little, too.

Suddenly, there was a scrambling sound.

"What's that?" Jack asked,

"Sounds like somebody's on the roof."

"Can they get in the house from there?"

"There's a chimney to the fireplace, but it's too small." He paused. "Uh, Jack, the coffee's ready. Do you want some?"

"Yeah, all right. Thanks."

"I keep my cigars in the fridge. Okay if I get one?"

"Okay."

"You want one?"

"None for me, I don't smoke."

"They're—"

"For Christ sakes, be quiet, will you? I gotta think!"

. . .

The telephone sounded. On the third ring, Jack walked over and picked it up.

"This is Sgt. John Brady, Los Angeles Sheriff's Office," said a voice. "Who is this?"

Jack hung up the phone.

"You got a couple of nice cars out there," he told Hoag. "I tried to hot-wire the T-bird, but lost my knife and couldn't get it done. Gimme the keys for it— the El Camino too."

The phone rang again. "You get it," Jack ordered.

It was Hoag's boss wondering if he was coming to work. "No, not right now," answered Hoag. He started to explain that there was a man holding a gun on him when Jack motioned for him to hang up. He did so.

"What's this all about?" asked Hoag. "You said you killed some people?"

"Boy, I wish I knew," Jack said. "The cops followed us into a gas station about five miles back, I guess. It must have been something to do with a hassle my partner got into earlier. Anyway, they got out with guns. We had to shoot it out. We got 'em all. I think there was four of them."

"You're so young, Jack," Hoag said. "How did you get into all this? I mean, what you're doing is wrong. What you've done is wrong. What about your parents? What would they....?"

"Shit! What parents? I don't even know if I ever had any. You know, after I got out of the joint in Tallahassee, I went back to North Carolina and tried to find out who my parents were. I couldn't even do that. Hell, nobody knows."

"That's too bad. Every...." The phone interrupted. Jack picked up the receiver.

"This is Sgt. Brady of the L. A. Sheriff's Office. How is everything in there?"

"Fine," said Jack sarcastically. "Everything's just fine. We're just sitting here watching the sun come up."

"Why don't you come on out and we'll talk about this?" Brady asked in a soothing voice.

"Nope! I'll stay here."

"What about Mr. Hoag?" asked Brady. "Can he come out?"

"Nope! He'll stay too, till I decide what to do."

"Come on," Brady said, "there are at least a hundred officers out here. You aren't going to get away. There's no sense in getting somebody hurt."

"Nobody will get hurt unless one of those hundred officers does something stupid!"

"What happened earlier tonight?" the sergeant asked.

"Well, I don't rightly know. They stopped us. We were ready; they weren't. One of them got real careless, so I wasted him. Did you get my partner?"

"Talbert?"

"Uh, yeah."

"They picked him up a few minutes ago. He gave up."

"I want to talk to him."

"Come on out, and we'll let you do that."

"Naw, you bring him here."

"I can't," Brady explained. "He got hurt. He's in the hospital."

"Get him on the phone."

"What?"

"Goddammit! I said get him on the phone! Get me his number so I can call, or have him call me!" He slammed down the receiver. "Oh shit! They got Bobby," he murmured, half to himself. "It's just me now—all by my lonesome."

In a few minutes the phone rang. Once more Jack picked it up.

"This is Deputy Scoval calling from the jail ward of the USC Medical Center. Hold on, please."

"Hello, Jack."

"Talbert?"

"Yeah."

"How are you? Are you hurt?"

"Not too good, my throat hurts. I got hit in the chest."

"Did you get it in the shoot-out?"

"No—later."

"I'm thinking of popping it off."

"I don't blame you, Jack. I wish I'd gotten one in the head myself."

"I'm just trying to make up my mind to do it. All I need is time to get up my nerve. Then I'm going to pop it off."

"I guess that might be the best thing to do."

"Well, you don't sound too good. I'll let you go."

"Okay, Jack."

"I don't want to go back to jail. As soon as I work up to it, I'm going to blow the top of my head off."

After a long pause, Davis said softly, "Jack, I wish you wouldn't."

"I'll see you, buddy." He hung up the phone.

It immediately rang again. This time it was Don Chamberlain of radio station KNEW in Oakland. "Sir, I know the situation down there and am just wondering what you plan to do," came the obviously professional voice through the earpiece.

How the hell had this disc jockey from the Bay Area gotten involved? "Nothing, I just want a few minutes to myself before I die. That's all."

"Why do you think you have to go that way?" Chamberlain asked.

"Well, I've been in prison before, and I don't want to go back again. And I figure it's better for me to do it myself than to let them do it for me."

"Of course, if you are held in California, you know, there hasn't been an execution here in a long time."

"Nobody has killed three or four Highway Patrolmen in a long time either!"

"Yes, but if you had a good attorney, they could put the thing off for several years, and there's a pretty good chance you could come out with your life."

"I wouldn't expect so." Once more he replaced the receiver. He turned to Hoag, "You go on out now. Tell them that I just want to be left alone for a while. I want to think this thing out."

Jack got up from the table and followed Hoag to the front door. As it was opened, he could see at least three patrol cars in the driveway and the roofs of several others over the brush on the hill. A half a dozen uniformed officers were partially visible, some concealing themselves to the rear of the cars, others crouched behind trees and rocks.

"Look at that silly bastard behind the bush." Jack pointed. "I could shoot right through it." As Hoag started out the door, Jack stopped him. "Here, take this." He reached into his pocket and pulled out a one hundred dollar bill. "I won't be needing it."

"Are you sure you want to go through with this?"

"I'm sure," Jack said as he closed the door.

Alone...just him against the whole frigging bunch. Well, he'd been alone before. Most of his life. And he'd survived. Been through hell, but he'd survived.

He sat down on the floor in the hallway with his back against the wall. He pulled the pistol from his belt and laid it on the carpet next to him. The shotgun was cradled in his lap.

Yes, he'd always survived, but was survival the most important thing? He could survive now, but it would mean going back. Nope, survival wasn't *that* important. He looked around the house. He didn't fit. Not in this kind of house— not in this kind of world.

Too bad he couldn't have been born a few years back when the important things weren't how much schooling or how good a job you had. When what mattered was how good you were with your fists. How tough. How brave. You didn't have to live in a nice house to be somebody. You weren't measured by what you owned. Hell, you didn't have to own a thing. You lived off the land and were respected for it.

The phone began to ring—long, plaintive peals that seemed to gain in intensity. Jack ignored them.

Dee Mauldin popped into his mind. Strange that he would think of her now. He wondered if she would read about all this. Probably not—not way back in Winston-Salem. She had been the only woman in his life. He'd known her less than a month, but he could tell that she cared for him. Really cared. It could have been nice if he'd found a job and not got screwed up by that bitch foster mother and had to leave.

Dee had loved to talk to him. They'd talked about life. About problems. About survival. Even though she was young and had been kind of a hick, coming from a small town and all, she had a good head on her shoulders. She had figured him out right away. Once she had called him an angry young man and accused him of taking on the whole world, one person at a time. Like she said, life was mixed up like clothes in a dryer. She was gone now. So was Bobby—the only other person he felt close to. Going back to the joint. Jack wouldn't go along this time.

"You, in there! Twining!" a voice bellowed from a loud speaker or bull horn. "CAN YOU HEAR ME?"

Again, Jack paid no heed to the effort to disturb his thoughts.

"It's now twenty after nine," the shouting continued. "You have until ten o'clock to come out! Put your guns down and come out the front door. At ten sharp, we will come in after you. Do you hear me?" The message was repeated.

Jack got up, went to the bathroom and relieved himself. The face that peered back at him from the mirror was strange. Almost two days' growth of beard. The mustache he was starting was matted and blood streaked. His hair was in wild disarray, not neatly combed as was his habit. A prison habit. The wound on his forehead... It looked like there was a bullet fragment lodged just under the skin. The eyes... Did they look that way because of what they had witnessed within the past twelve hours? Or was that thirty-four years of pain, hunger and frustration trying to surface? Was there a hint of fear visible at the corners of the mouth? That mouth that had continuously sneered at authority. Jack attempted a sneer and let it fade into a look of resolution.

He went back into the hall and sat down in the same place and position.

At 10:02, he once again heard the voice on the loud speaker. "Come out! This is your last chance!"

Jack was thinking about his parents...parents he had never known. Perhaps he would meet up with them someday.

• • •

At precisely 10:10, the front picture window of the Hoag home was shattered by a CN 115 exploding gas grenade. Simultaneously, tear gas grenades were tossed into two bedroom windows. The thick smoke and powerful fumes quickly spread through the house.

• • •

Jack sat motionless on the floor of the hall leading to the kitchen...the shotgun tightly gripped in his hands.

After approximately sixty seconds, two members of the Sheriff's assault team, wearing gas masks and body armor, rushed the front door. Two more kicked in the rear door. They were armed with shotguns and pistols. They went in, firing blindly ahead of them. They couldn't see because of the density of the smoke and gas. Realizing their vulnerability, the deputies hastily retreated.

• • •

Again, it was silent. Jack sat quietly, not even bothering to think. He was alone again.

Five minutes passed. Jack could hear them coming again. He put the muzzle of the shotgun under his chin, reached down with his left thumb and pushed the trigger.

EPILOGUE

The aftermath of the Newhall Incident, as it came to be known, was similar to that of any minor disaster. The news quickly spread throughout California, then nationwide, and then to the world at large. For the first two days it made front page headlines in most major newspapers.

Readers were stunned that this type of thing could happen in a civilized land. Their shock was dissipated a few columns later as they read about an earthquake in the Himalayas which had claimed 400 lives. Within days, the aborted Apollo 13 Moonshot replaced the Newhall tragedy in the words of newscasters and in the minds of the viewers.

Yet public response to the incident was different from that of many tragedies. Perhaps because of the waste of the lives of four young officers. Perhaps out of sympathy for their families. Possibly because of a collective sense of guilt.

Whatever the reason, within three days, nearly five thousand people sent letters to CHP headquarters. Many contained donations which totaled a hundred thousand dollars for the four widows and nine orphaned children.

Probably spurred by the public's interest, the California press resumed carrying articles concerning the incident. These broadened into features on the men who were killed, on their families, and on the Highway Patrol. Media examined the enforcement tactics taught at the Academy, the CHP's shooting policy, and felony arrest procedures. Reporters questioned the Patrol's wisdom in assigning virtually inexperienced officers as partners in such a critical location as the primary route into and out of the State's major city. Yet, for the most part, the media was fair, objective, and sensitive in its coverage.

One glaring example which differed was an article which appeared in a counterculture paper.

A VICTORY FOR THE PEOPLE

Four pigs were offed this past week...a victory for the people, a tactical example—moves of oppressed people for their ultimate attainment of liberation....

In the past, whenever there were shoot-outs or confrontations between pigs and the people, there was never any pig killed, one never died even in the face of such overwhelming evidence that no one could have lived. The pigs lived through the Watts rebellion where Niger's [sic] ruled the streets for days; the pigs further say that they suffered very few casualties in the midst of the sniper fire in Detroit. In every altercation between pigs and people, the pigs have always maintained that they held the upper hand or control of the situation throughout the 'disturbance'....

There are four dead pigs, killed by two men with guns...the pigs can and will die, but not from a wish and a prayer. Relate to pigs as men, less than men, rather as foul perverts, and see that bone, and they will bleed; they will die. When the hour of reckoning comes, as you move into the streets to fight for your survival, remember the lesson taught by this one simple sentence...

FOUR PIGS DEAD!
ALL POWER TO THE PEOPLE
TAKE THE STRUGGLE TO THE STREETS

Five hundred thousand police across the country could identify with the dangers of making a similar type enforcement stop, not knowing what to expect, often not knowing what to do. How could it have happened? they asked themselves. Four officers of one of the best-trained departments in the world gunned down by a couple of punks. Five thousand CHP officers asked the same questions. "Perhaps they were overconfident because of the lighted area and all the people around." "Gore and Frago knew a backup was coming; they must have let down their guard." "Pence and Alleyn may have been killed before they could get clear of their car." So the speculations went.

In addition to the massive criminal homicide investigation being carried out by the Los Angeles County Sheriff's Office, the California Highway Patrol launched its own in-depth inquiry to determine what, in fact, had occurred at Newhall. This investigation disclosed that in less than four minutes, a total of forty shots were fired. It disclosed that the officers had "overcommitted," had let the bad guys dictate the situation.

Events surrounding the Newhall incident were documented for training purposes in a slide presentation shown to law enforcement agencies across the nation. This has since been adopted as a part of the curriculum at the FBI National Academy at Quantico, Virginia. In later years, bullet proof vests and speed loaders, followed by semiautomatic pistols, would become issue gear on the Patrol.

For most of those involved, the tragedy carried on interminably. Officers Gore, Frago, Pence and Alleyn were eulogized and mourned in separate ceremonies in their individual home towns. A formal memorial ceremony was held in Newhall. For the latter occasion, hundreds of police officers from the Los Angeles Basin attended in full dress uniform. These same hundreds stood with lumps in their throats as taps was played bidding the four men a peaceful slumber.

After Jack Wright Twining took his own life during the siege at the Hoag residence, his body was transported to the L. A. County morgue for an autopsy. Because no one came to claim it during the next ninety days, it was buried in a pauper's grave at the Los Angeles City cemetery. No one had welcomed him into the world, few had cared for him in life, and none had mourned his departure.

Bobby Augustus Davis gave up his pretense at being Russell Talbert and was in the L. A. County jail charged with four counts of first-degree murder.

After a lengthy evidentiary hearing over the admissibility of items seized at the Ximino apartment which definitely tied him to the red Pontiac, Davis was ordered to stand trial in October 1970.

In the maximum-security unit of the County jail, a forty-four-year-old hippy named Charles Manson also was awaiting a murder trial. Manson and Davis, who befriended one another, concocted a scheme for escape. It involved chipping out several glass window blocks in their cell dormitory area. Once the blocks were removed, they planned to tie sheets and bedding together to permit climbing down to the street three stories below. When they were on the ground, a Manson follower was to pick them up in a car. The pair had several of the blocks loosened when another inmate told the jailers of the plan. Davis was caught red-handed chipping away at the mortar. Placed in solitary confinement, he blamed Manson for "ratting him off."

As ordered, the trial of the People of the State of California vs. Bobby Augustus Davis began on October 6, 1970 in the Los Angeles County Superior Court, with His Honor Judge L. Thaxton Hanson presiding. James B. Ideman, a Deputy District Attorney, prosecuted. Marvin Schwartz and Richard Plotin, Deputy Public Defenders, served as defense counsel. The trial was by jury and lasted twenty-three days.

Fifteen of those days were involved with taking evidence on the guilt phase and two with the penalty phase. There were 294 exhibits marked for identification and ninety-seven witnesses testified—among them the four widows.

In order for Davis to escape the first-degree murder charge, the defense used diminished capacity, a form of insanity, as the plea. The court appointed Dr. Nicholas Langner, a psychiatrist, to examine Davis. At Dr. Langner's request, a psychologist, Dr. Harry J. Rosenthal, also was appointed to examine the defendant.

Dr. Langner testified that by reason of his childhood situation (parental indifference), Bobby Davis could not control his anger and hostility and, if he became impatient, intolerant, or under the impression that he was threatened, he exploded. In those circumstances, Davis lacked the main ingredients for normal reaction, reason, logic and judgment. Dr. Rosenthal characterized Davis as a person of potentially superior intelligence who had never used that intelligence effectively. He said Bobby showed poor judgment and little emotional control under stress. All this was caused by the conditions of his boyhood—parental preference for the older sister Jeanette and the piling of affection on the physically deficient sister Geraldine.

In spite of the testimony of these experts, the prosecution prevailed. Deputy D. A. Ideman orchestrated a perfect case. He was assisted throughout by the chief Sheriff's Office homicide investigator, Sgt. John Brady. Together, they convinced the jury of five men and seven women that Bobby Augustus Davis deserved to die.

During the trial, evidence was introduced by the prosecution which implicated Davis in yet another killing. According to testimony given by a former accomplice, Jim Travis Ward, he and Davis had flown from Oklahoma to Brighton, Colorado, in June of 1963 in search of a score.

In the early morning hours of June 13, the pair had followed a waitress from a closing diner in hopes of robbing her of the daily receipts. They had tracked the woman to her home and gained entry by breaking in a side door. They were then accosted by her husband, George R. Barrett. In full view of the Barretts' thirteen-year-old daughter, Davis shot and killed Barrett with a .32 automatic pistol. Evidence was also introduced that Davis had in fact purchased a .32 caliber automatic pistol on June 12, 1963, from the U.S. Loan and Surplus Store in Ponca City, Oklahoma, for $17.50.

Of particular interest in this respect was that the thirteen-year-old, currently a twenty-year-old young woman residing in the California Bay area, had no conscious recollection of the killing of her father. Prosecutor Ideman, after being contacted by Ward (serving time in a Federal prison and hoping for a deal if he helped convict Davis) and after reviewing the Brighton, Colorado police reports, believed that perhaps the Barrett girl had repressed the memory of that night from her consciousness.

Under hypnosis, Miss Barrett did recall the circumstances of her father's death but was unable to positively identify Bobby Davis as the perpetrator.

To this day, Brighton, Colorado, authorities list the murder of George R. Barrett as unsolved. But they have placed a detention hold on Davis should he ever be released by California authorities.

In pronouncing sentence on the outwardly unemotional appearing defendant, Judge L. Thaxton Hanson stated, in part:

> **Bobby Augustus Davis, for the crimes of murder in the first degree which you stand convicted, it is the judgment and sentence of the Court that you be put to death in the manner prescribed by law....**
>
> **Upon affirmance of this judgment on appeal, this court will set a date for your execution. Thereafter, the Warden of the State Prison of the State of California at San Quentin is ordered to execute you and put you to death by the administration of lethal gas in the manner prescribed by the laws of the State of California. This judgment is to apply to each count of the information....**
>
> **In addition, this trial court is aware that cases urging the abolition of the death sentence are presently pending before the high courts. This trial court can visualize no rational constitutional basis for abolition of the death penalty, being a legislative function, but in the event that some high court should, after 200 years, by sweeping judicial legislation, suddenly find a constitutional basis for abolishing the death penalty, it is the recommendation of this court, based upon all the evidence that was before this court during trial, that if this should be reduced to life sentence, that these life sentences run consecutively.**
>
> **The defendant and his partner in this case have snuffed out over two to three hundred years of human life, these four officers.**
>
> **There is also evidence of killing another man, Mr. Barrett, who was sound asleep in his home until he was invaded in the early hours of the morning and within a few minutes he was mortally wounded and shot, as the evidence shows, by this defendant, another fifty years of human life snuffed out.**
>
> **The defendant's attitude during the trial has shown no remorse.**
>
> **In addition to that, the defendant was attempted to be rehabilitated for some six years in a prison. As soon as he was released on parole, he violated his parole and started the crime spree which ended in this trial.**
>
> **Therefore, it is the recommendation, in the event that the death penalty should be abolished, that these run consecutively and it is the recommendation of this court that if that should come to pass, that this defen-**

dant, if released on the streets, from what this court had heard in this trial, could well kill again,...he should...no longer be allowed for the rest of his life to walk a free man on the streets.

• • •

In the mid-sixties, Robert Page Anderson, while robbing a San Diego pawn shop, killed the owner and shot at three others including a police officer. He too was convicted of murder in the first degree, but after eight years of appeals, the Supreme Court determined that the California death penalty was cruel and unusual and thus unconstitutional. This resulted in the setting aside of the execution of forty-eight individuals on California's death row. Bobby Augustus Davis was one of them.

Shortly thereafter, Davis was removed from death row at San Quentin and transferred to the maximum security prison at Folsom, California. His continued recalcitrant behavior has resulted in subsequent transfers to Cochran, a level four institution, and more recently to the notorious Pelican Bay Prison, a State run replica of Alcatraz, established for the most hard core of the inmate population.

In the meantime, as head-shaven members of the Manson family accosted passersby in front of L. A.'s Hall of Justice, another young man also spent time on the city sidewalks. During the months following the shooting, Walter Frago's grief-stricken older brother Tom became mentally disoriented. He left his job as an instructor at Soledad State Prison and traveled to Los Angeles. There he took to wandering the streets in search of Walt. Finally, in despair, he took his own life by means of a four-inch revolver. In less than a year, Gus and Rose Frago had lost two sons.

In less than four minutes Roger Gore, Walter Frago, James Pence and George Alleyn had had their futures brutally canceled. They would not live to share the national pride of the shuttle program. They'd not hear of the end of the Vietnam conflict or European detente or the falling of the Berlin Wall and failure of the USSR. To them, through eternity, Watergate would be just an unheralded hotel in the District of Columbia. Test tube babies and cloning would happen outside their awareness. Hand-held computers, fax machines, electronic TV games, consumer price coding, and automatic teller machines would be unknown. They'd not know about the energy crisis, Skylab, cellular telephones, or women on the Highway Patrol.

Perhaps the loss was greatest for the four widows whose hearts suffered scars that would be wrenched open each time they saw a black-and-white patrol car, saw a newspaper article on the CHP, or an insensitive acquaintance related the tale of a traffic ticket. Mention of the word Newhall would conjure up dark memories, fostering nightmarish recollections. Did they recover?

Each has pushed her pain aside, picked up her shattered life and started over. To those around the women, the tragedy is seemingly past. Still, they harbor a grief that will never leave them.

And what of the children? Their "real" daddy would become forever a vague memory refreshed only by the picture in the living room of a serious young man in a uniform hat. Serious? Perhaps. Idealistic? Definitely.

From mid-1968 to April 5, 1970, these men had experienced their "one brief shining moment."

It must be left to psychologists and sociologists to speculate as to why six young men, five of whom had similar middle class backgrounds and upbringings, were placed in the position of shooting it out in a service station parking lot.

California Governor Ronald Reagan capsulized the importance of the Newhall incident when he stated:

If anything worthwhile comes of this tragedy, it should be the realization by every citizen that often the only thing that stands between them and their losing everything they hold dear...is the man wearing a badge.

Time and developers' dreams have all but erased the location where the confrontation occurred. J's Restaurant has been replaced by a Marie Callender's, and the Standard station has moved diagonally across the intersection, transformed into a modern Chevron with a mini-mart and a dozen gas islands. A Hilton Garden Motel covers the killing grounds.

Daily, tens of thousands of motorists take the Henry Mayo off-ramp from Interstate 5, cross the Old Highway and continue west on what has been renamed Magic Mountain Parkway. Few on their way to or from the family theme park have any idea of the tragedy which occurred less than 200 feet from the intersection.

In the evening, when traffic on the freeway drops off, the shrill screams from the Colossus roller coaster could be mistaken for the cries of outrage and injustice that linger in the minds and hearts of those who remember, and the angry clatter of the wheels could be echoes of the shots fired that night a third of a century ago.

ABOUT THE AUTHORS

John Anderson's career with the California
Highway Patrol spanned thirty-three years. In 1965
he served in Los Angeles during the Watts riots. In
1984 Anderson oversaw athlete security during the
Los Angeles Olympic Games.

For three years he was the director of the CHP
Academy in West Sacramento, California. He spent
a year in Washington D.C. testifying before con-
gressional committees on evaluations for the National Highway Traffic Safety Administration.

As CHP Central Division chief, he commanded
700 uniformed officers and 300 support personnel.

Anderson has a criminal justice degree from
California State University, Sacramento and a
master's degree in public administration from
Golden Gate University.

In 1998 he was elected Sheriff of Madera
County, California. Anderson lives with his wife
Kathy in the Sierra Nevada foothills near Yosemite
National Park.

Marsh Cassady is the author of more than forty
published books including novels, biography, short
story and drama collections. He has a Ph.D. in
theatre and has had eighteen stage and audio plays
produced. He currently lives on the Pacific Coast
in Baja California.

To order another copy of this book, please call
1-800-497-4909